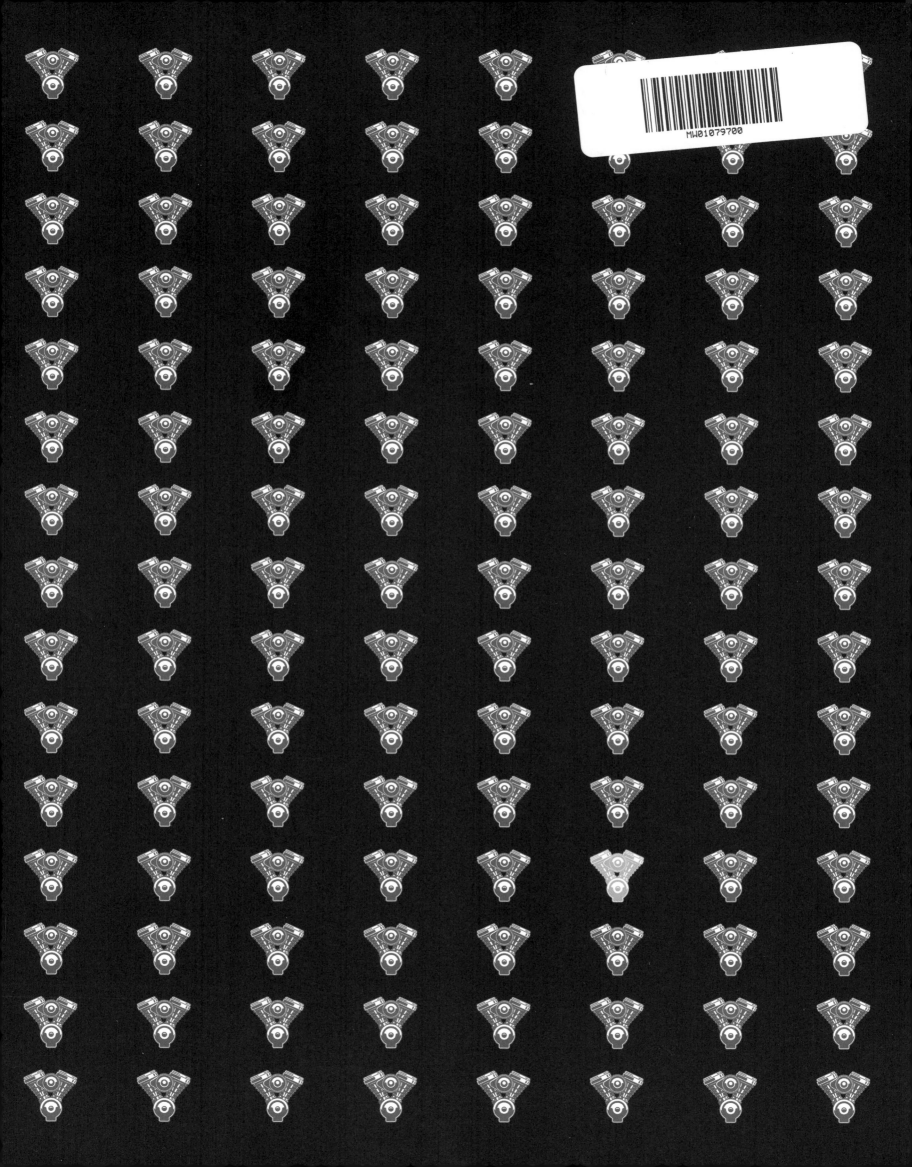

THE
Harley- Davidson
-BOOK-

teNeues

TWO WORDS.
TWO WHEELS.
TWO CYLINDERS.
LIMITLESS FREEDOM.

It sounds adventurous. For most people, the ears are the first point of contact with a Harley-Davidson motorcycle. It's the sound of adventure. The unique experience of that low-frequency, staccato sound from a distance growing into a tremendous roar. This aural experience is offered only by the powerful motorcycles from Milwaukee. They normally run on 45-degree V2 engines that give them both that sound and their practically legendary reputation.

Buying a Harley-Davidson motorcycle automatically makes you part of a large family, a community that cultivates the American dream of freedom. A community that dreams of the "outlaw" image of the past. A community that finds itself coming together at countless international events, completely separated from everyday obligations and conventions. Willie G. Davidson, retired head designer and grandson of the founder, sums it up by saying, "Harley-Davidson sells an attitude toward life. The motorcycle is complementary."

In this book, we'll show you the power and beauty of the engines as well as the elegance and strength of these machines from the shores of Lake Michigan. We'll also take a look at the rich and vibrant history of the unique Harley-Davidson lifestyle. The Harley-Davidson Book is a tribute to the wonderful Flatheads, Knuckleheads, Panheads, Shovels, Evolutions and the modern engines with fuel injection. It's a bow to the people who created this legend. There's just one thing we can't provide in this book: The unique sound of a Harley-Davidson.

Yours – Ihr – Bien à vous

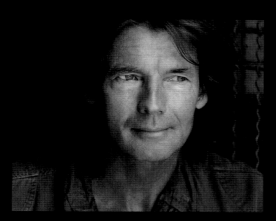

MICHAEL KÖCKRITZ
EDITOR-IN-CHIEF

Es klingt abenteuerlich! In vielen Fällen erfolgt die erste Begegnung mit einer Harley-Davidson über das Gehör, über diesen abenteuerlichen Klang. Das einzigartige Erlebnis, wenn das tieffrequente, arrhythmische Geräusch aus der Ferne zu einem gewaltigen Getöse anschwillt – diesen Hörgenuss bieten nur die mächtigen Motorräder aus Milwaukee. Gespeist vom typischen 45-Grad-V2-Motor, der ihnen diesen Sound und den beinahe mythischen Ruf verleiht.

Käufer einer Harley-Davidson werden automatisch zu Mitgliedern einer großen Familie, einer Community, die den amerikanischen Traum von der Freiheit pflegt. Die vom Outlaw-Image vergangener Zeiten träumt. Und die sich zu unzähligen internationalen Veranstaltungen zusammenfindet, losgelöst von alltäglichen Pflichten und Konventionen. Willie G. Davidson, Chefdesigner im Ruhestand und Enkel des Firmengründers, bringt es auf den Punkt: „Harley-Davidson verkauft ein Lebensgefühl. Das Motorrad gibt es kostenlos dazu."

In diesem Buch zeigen wir daher nicht nur die Kraft und Schönheit der Motoren, die Eleganz und Stärke der Maschinen vom Lake Michigan. Wir spüren auch und vor allem in opulenten, bilderreichen Geschichten dem einzigartigen Harley-Davidson-Lifestyle nach. „The Harley-Davidson Book" ist Hommage an die wunderbaren Flatheads, Knuckleheads, Panheads, die Shovels, Evolutions und die modernen Einspritzer, eine Verneigung vor den Menschen, die diesen Mythos erschaffen haben. Nur eines können wir an dieser Stelle leider nicht bieten: den unnachahmlichen Sound einer Harley-Davidson.

Cela paraît bizarre, mais il n'est pas rare que la première rencontre avec une Harley-Davidson passe par l'oreille. Cette sonorité incroyable qui génère une sensation unique lorsque retentit au loin un bruit tout en fréquences basses et en arythmie, qui enfle et se transforme en un vacarme puissant. Seules les puissantes machines de Milwaukee produisent ce bruit jouissif, celui du moteur V2 à 45 degrés symbole de la marque, qui lui confère ce son unique et sa réputation quasi-mystique.

Acheter une Harley-Davidson, c'est devenir automatiquement membre d'une grande famille, d'une communauté qui entretient le rêve américain de liberté. C'est rêver de l'époque révolue des hors-la-loi. C'est participer aux innombrables rassemblements internationaux, libéré des contraintes et des conventions du quotidien. Willie G. Davidson, chef designer à la retraite et petit-fils du fondateur de l'entreprise, l'exprime bien : « Harley-Davidson vend un art de vivre. La moto, elle est offerte gratuitement, en prime. »

Dans ce livre, nous ne parlerons donc pas seulement de la puissance et de la beauté des moteurs, ou de l'élégance et de la force des machines du lac Michigan. Nous raconterons aussi des histoires riches et imagées pour retrouver les traces de ce qui caractérise l'esprit Harley-Davidson. Le Harley-Davidson Book est un hommage aux merveilleuses Flatheads, Knuckleheads, Panheads, Shovels, Evolutions et aux modèles modernes à injection, une occasion de s'incliner devant les femmes et les hommes qui ont créé le mythe. Il restera une chose que nous ne pouvons pas offrir : le son inimitable d'une Harley-Davidson.

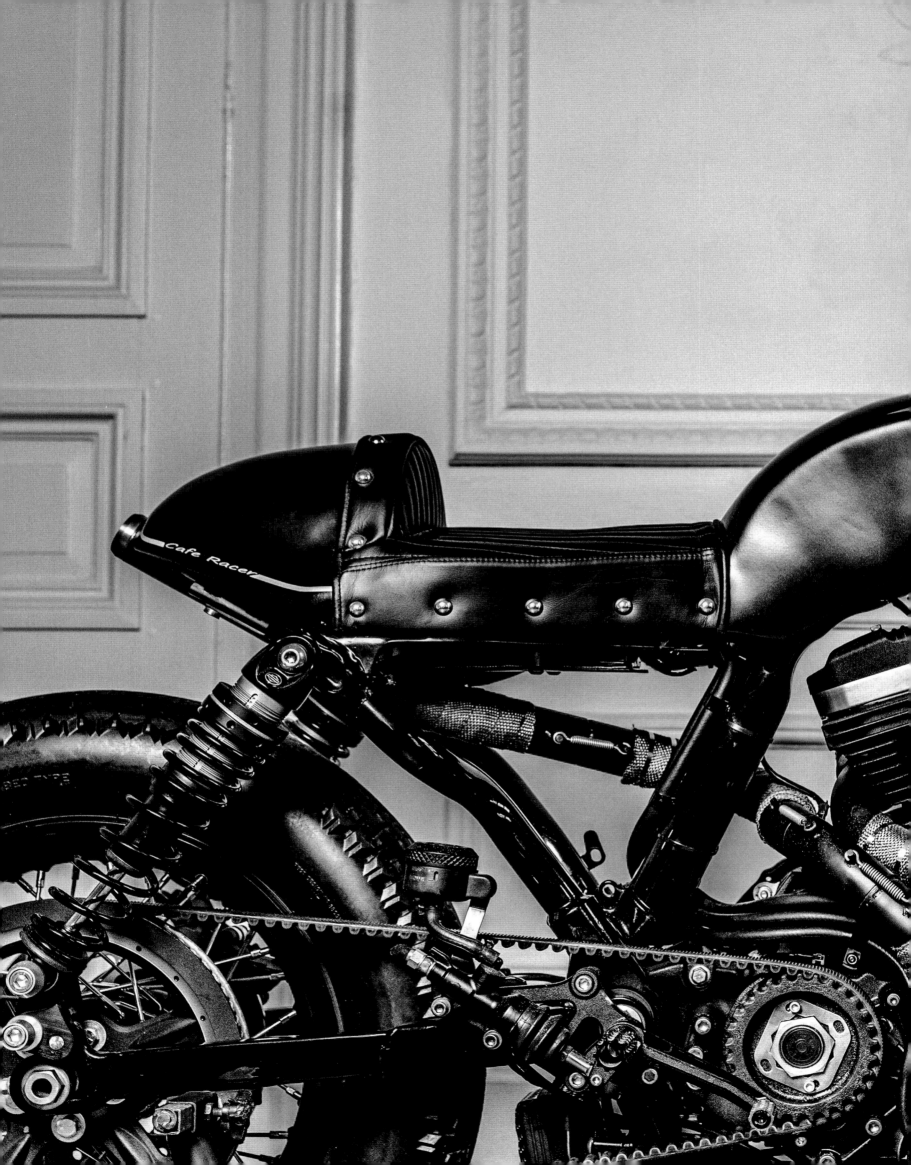

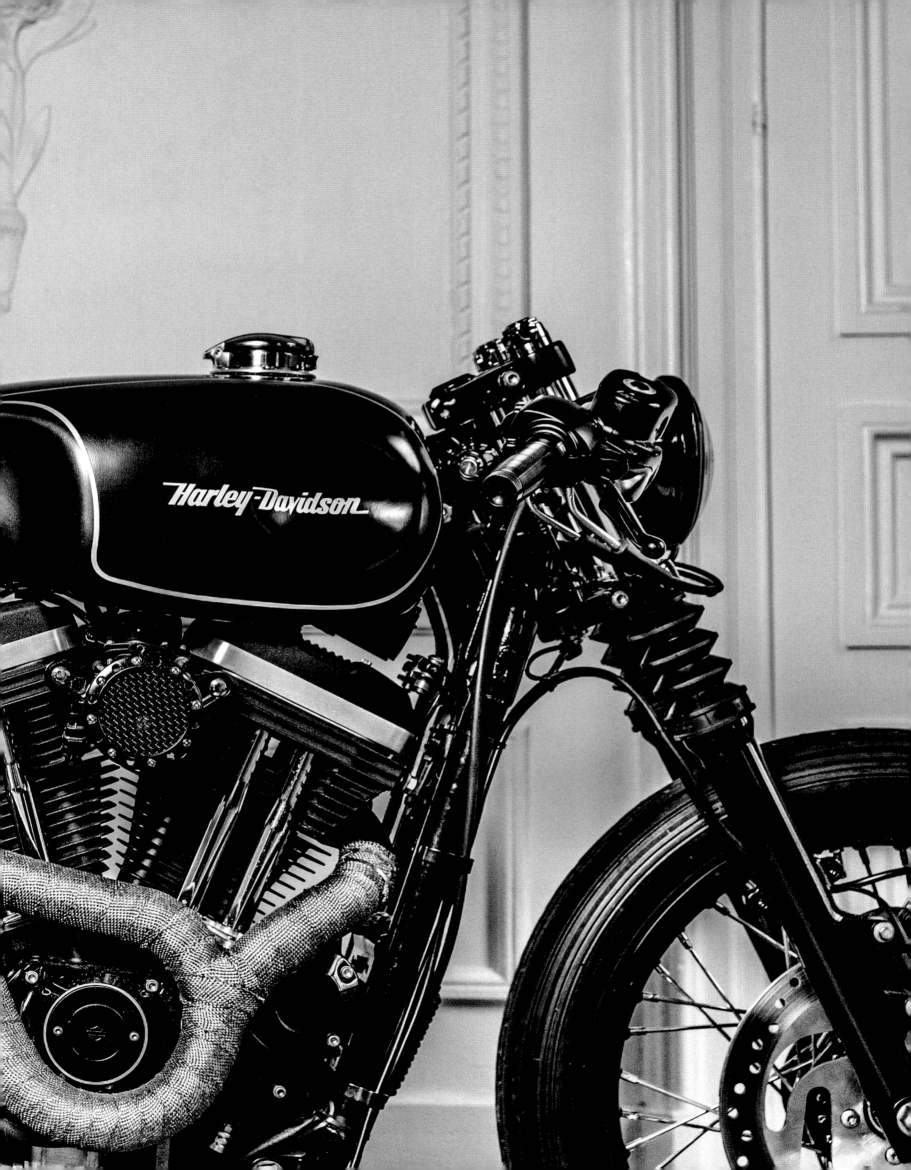

HISTORY

RACING

EVENTS

CUSTOMIZING

LIFESTYLE

ART & GIRLS

Da Guru

After studying media design at the Bauhaus, he decided to work as a freelance photographer. Mainly to be able to travel. That was ten years ago. Ever since, he has been on his way all around the world. On his FXR Evolution. The first H-D that he has owned. He will never get rid of it.

Dirk Mangartz

Former editor-in chief of the German motor-cycle magazine "Custombike," author and co-author of various books on motorcycles. He develops and sells motorcycle accessories. His passion for vehicles in general, and for motorcycles in particular, has always been his consistent driving force.

Philipp Wente

Freelance photographer. Author of the German cult motor vehicle magazine "ramp." He was already cruising on the asphalt on two wheels in diapers. On his Puky kick scooter emblazoned in racing orange. The one with the cool pennant on the front fender. Today, he prefers his Ducati Pantah and his stripped H-D Early Shovel FLH.

Götz Göppert

Loves his job. Lives on his passion for photography and everything that has wheels. And off his travels, which he often under-takes on motorcycles, including customized and one-of-a-kind models. Most of all, he has a fascination with modified prewar H-Ds and their fittingly dressed riders.

Sven Wedemeyer

The journalist and photographer works for renowned magazines, agencies and manufac-turers. His reports grant unusual insight into the culture of mobility. For this book, the motorcycle junkie has salvaged special trea-sures of the customizing scene and sheds light on the sporting heritage out of Milwaukee.

Laurent Nivalle

You don't need to tell Laurent Nivalle that the most thrilling tales can often be found on the street. His pictures convey entire road movies, preferably on two or four wheels but recently in the world of fashion too. A native Parisian, he studied art and product design at the École Boulle, giving him a métier that he practices as Art Director for DS/Citroën with the same passion as he dedicates to his

FROM BACKYARD GARAGE TO GLOBAL ICON.

What do Arthur Davidson and his childhood friend William S. Harley have in common with Bill Gates and Paul Allen (Microsoft), Steve Jobs and Steve Wosniak (Apple), Larry Page and Sergey Brin (Google) and even William Hewlett and David Packard? They got their start together in a garage. And, within a very short time, they created a global company worth billions.

AUS DER HEIMISCHEN GARAGE ZUR WELTWEITEN IKONE.

Was haben Arthur Davidson und sein Schulfreund William S. Harley mit Bill Gates und Paul Allen (Microsoft), Steve Jobs und Steve Wozniak (Apple), Larry Page und Sergey Brin (Google) sowie William Hewlett und David Packard gemeinsam? Sie haben zu zweit in einer Garage begonnen. Und innerhalb kürzester Zeit einen milliardenschweren Weltkonzern auf die Beine gestellt.

DU GARAGE D'UNE MAISON À L'ICÔNE MONDIALE.

Quels sont les points communs entre les duos célèbres que sont Arthur Davidson et son copain de classe William S. Harley, Bill Gates et Paul Allen (Microsoft), Steve Jobs et Steve Wosniak (Apple), Larry Page et Sergey Brin (Google) ou encore William Hewlett et David Packard ? Ils ont tous commencé à deux dans un garage. Et créé en un temps très court de grands groupes mondiaux.

FROM THE BACKYARD TO THE LARGEST MOTORCYCLE MANUFACTURER IN THE WORLD

The United States at the end of the nineteenth century provided a virtually perfect location for creative inventors. Countless car plants began springing up in the eastern half of the country in 1902, seeking to bring mobility to the American market. In the industrial city of Milwaukee, two schoolboy pals, William S. Harley and Arthur Davidson, set to work realizing the dream of making their own motorcycles. Under challenging conditions, the pair worked out of a shed

Für kreative Erfinder waren die USA im ausklingenden 19. Jahrhundert ein geradezu idealer Ort. Ab 1902 sprossen vor allem im weit entwickelten Osten viele Fahrzeugfabriken aus dem Boden, um die inneramerikanische Mobilmachung nach vorne zu treiben. In der Industriestadt Milwaukee machten sich zwei Schulfreunde, William S. Harley und Arthur Davidson, daran, ihren Traum von einer eigenen Motorradfabrikation zu realisieren. Unter abenteuerlichen

En cette fin de 19ᵉ siècle, les États-Unis sont un endroit presque idéal pour les inventeurs et les créateurs. À partir de 1902, surtout dans l'est développé, de nombreuses usines d'automobiles poussent comme des champignons pour propulser la mobilisation intérieure vers l'avant. Dans la ville industrielle de Milwaukee, deux amis d'école, William S. Harley et Arthur Davidson, décident de réaliser leur rêve : fabriquer leur propre moto. Dans des conditions difficiles, installés dans

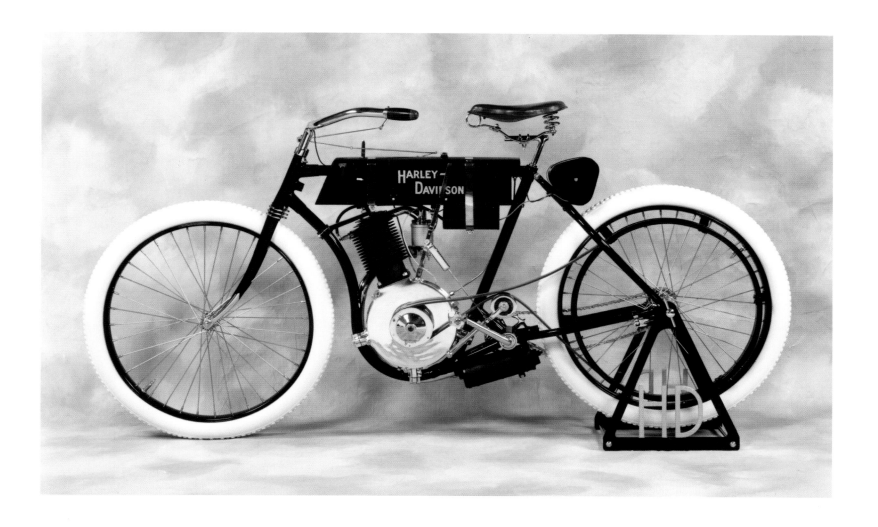

covering scarcely 20 square meters to develop a single-cylinder, four-stroke engine with 167 cc displacement. They put this first engine in a reinforced bicycle frame. The first series-production model from 1903 used a refined IOE valve control with air valve and now 405 cc at 3 HP. Harley and Davidson used a loop-frame pattern made in-house that provided significantly more stability.

The real sensation came in 1909 with the introduction of a 45° V-twin engine—the same design that defines the brand to this day. The 5D model delivered 7 HP, enabling an impressive top speed of 105 km/h. The powerful, dependable two-cylinder motorcycle proved especially adept when combined with a side car. Two-cylinder Harleys also quickly became favorites in board track and dirt track racing. The first racer models were followed by the Sixty-One featuring a pocket valve engine and, in 1915, the lightning-fast OHV eight-valve racer.

Bedingungen in einem hölzernen, kaum 20 Quadratmeter großen Schuppen entwickelten die beiden einen kleinen Einzylinder-Viertaktmotor mit 167 ccm. Dieses erste Aggregat pflanzten sie zunächst in verstärkte Fahrradrahmen. Für das erste Serienmodell von 1903 mit weiterentwickelter IOE-Ventilsteuerung samt Schnüffelventil und nun 405 ccm bei 3 PS verwendeten Harley und Davidson einen selbst gefertigten Schleifenrahmen, der wesentlich stabiler ausfiel.

V-TWIN ENGINE

une petite remise en bois d'à peine 20 m², les deux amis conçoivent un petit moteur monocylindre quatre-temps de 167 cm³. Ils greffent d'abord ce premier moteur sur des cadres de vélo renforcés. Pour le premier modèle de série sorti en 1903, doté d'un moteur de 400 cm³ développant 3 ch et d'une distribution IOE à soupape d'admission d'air, Harley et Davidson utilisent un cadre berceau nettement plus résistant, qu'ils ont fabriqué eux-mêmes.

Mais la véritable sensation sera en 1909 le lancement d'un bicylindre en V à 45°, aujourd'hui encore symbole de la marque. Le modèle 5D avait une puissance de 7 ch et autorisait une vitesse maximale royale de 105 km/h. Cette moto bicylindre à la fois fiable et puissante fit ses preuves surtout dans sa version side-car. Très vite, les Harleys à deux cylindres sont appréciées dans les courses de board track et de dirt track. Les premiers modèles de course sont suivis de la Sixty-One à moteur Pocket-Valve et, à partir de 1915, de la rapide Racer à huit soupapes en tête (OHV).

17

The once-tiny company grew into a huge business almost overnight. By 1914, the company had moved into a six-story brick building on present-day Juneau Ave. in Milwaukee. With 2,400 employees and an annual output of 35,000 motorcycles, Harley-Davidson was the largest motorcycle manufacturer in the world.

The 1200 cc JD model introduced in 1922 was succeeded by the luxury VL model with up to 28 HP in 1930—not the ideal situation for the start of the Great Depression. But the brand was able to weather these difficult years with its rugged U models, affectionately dubbed "big flatheads" by fans.

Die eigentliche Sensation sollte 1909 die Einführung eines V-Zweizylindermotors mit 45° Zylinderwinkel sein, wie er noch heute das Gesicht der Marke prägt. Das Modell 5D leistete 7 PS und ermöglichte eine Höchstgeschwindigkeit von stattlichen 105 km/h. Vor allem mit Seitenwagen bewährte sich das zuverlässige und kraftvolle Zweizylinder-Motorrad. Schnell wurden die Zweizylinder-Harleys auch bei Board-Track- und Dirt-Track-Rennen beliebt. Auf die ersten Rennmodelle folgten die Sixty-One mit Pocket-Valve-Motor und ab 1915 pfeilschnelle ohv-Achtventil-Racer (overhead valves, hängende Ventile).

Der einstmals winzige Betrieb war kometenhaft zu einem großen Konzern aufgestiegen. Bereits 1914 zog die Company in ein sechsstöckiges Backsteingebäude an der heutigen Juneau Avenue in Milwaukee. Mit 2 400 Arbeitern und einem Jahresausstoß von 35 000 Motorrädern galt Harley-Davidson als die größte Motorradfabrik der Welt.

L'entreprise minuscule des débuts connaît alors une progression phénoménale et s'est muée en grand groupe. Dès 1914, la société emménage dans un bâtiment en briques de six étages, située sur l'actuelle Juneau Ave à Milwaukee. Avec 2 400 ouvriers et une production annuelle de 35 000 motos, Harley-Davidson est alors considéré comme le plus grand constructeur de motos du monde.

Le modèle JD 1200 cm³ présenté en 1922 sera suivie en 1930 de la luxueuse VL avec ses 28 ch, pas un modèle idéal en ce début de crise économique mondiale.

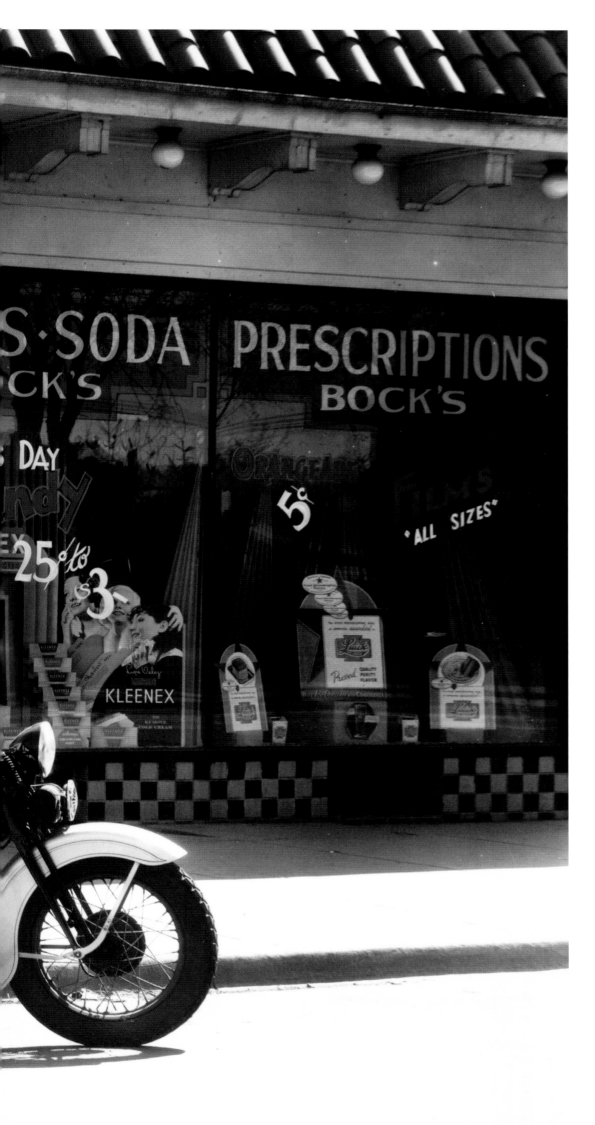

The middle of the 1930s brought the three-wheeled Servi-car for police use as well as for dealers and commercial enterprises. It used a hand-shifted three-gear transmission and enjoyed immense popularity.

Auf das 1922 vorgestellte JD-Modell mit 1 200 ccm folgte 1930 die luxuriöse VL mit bis zu 28 PS – nicht gerade ideal für die Zeit der Weltwirtschaftskrise. Doch mit den robusten U-Modellen, von ihren Fans liebevoll „Big Flathead" getauft, konnte sich die Marke auch über diese schweren Jahre retten. Mitte der 1930er gab es dann für die Polizei wie auch für Händler und Handwerksbetriebe das dreirädrige „Servi-Car" mit Drei-Gang-Handschaltung, welches sich großer Beliebtheit erfreute.

Mais grâce aux robustes modèles U, que les amateurs avaient affectueusement baptisés « Big-Flathead », la marque parvient à se sortir de ces années difficiles.
Au milieu des années trente, la police ainsi que les commerçants et artisans apprécient beaucoup le tricycle « Servi-Car » à boîte manuelle à trois rapports.

FROM FLATHEAD TO SHOVELHEAD TO TWIN CAM ENGINE

PHOTOS: HARLEY-DAVIDSON

FLATHEAD

In 1936, Harley-Davidson was at the forefront of the international market for two-wheeled transportation with its new OHV model series. The E and F models, called knuckleheads due to the knuckle-like look of the rocker boxes, were true technical marvels. They featured a streamlined design able to reach up to 160 km/h. Alongside the knuckleheads, the unassuming side-valve flatheads remained part of the product selection. The 750 cc class gained outstanding fame as the WLA military model. Some 88,000 of these indestructible dispatch motorcycles rode through the Second World War. Harley-Davidson had become an important supplier of military hardware.

1936 setzte sich Harley-Davidson mit einer neuen ohv-Modellreihe an die Spitze des internationalen Zweiradangebots. Die aufgrund ihrer knöchelförmigen Zylinderköpfe „Knucklehead" genannten E- und F-Modelle galten als technisches Meisterwerk. Sie waren stromlinienförmig gestaltet und erreichten

En 1936, Harley-Davidson lance une gamme de modèles à soupapes en tête qui le propulse à la pointe de l'offre internationale de deux-roues. Baptisés « Knucklehead » en raison de la forme en poing serré des cache-culbuteurs, les modèles E et F sont considérés comme des chefs d'œuvre techniques. Grâce à leurs lignes aérodynamiques, ces motos peuvent atteindre 160 km/h. En parallèle, les « flatheads » à soupapes latérales, moins évoluées techniquement, figurent toujours dans la gamme. La 750 connait une renommée extraordinaire dans sa version militaire WLA. Durant la Seconde Guerre mondiale, 88 000 de ces machines indestructibles ont servi de véhicules d'estafettes. Harley-Davidson est alors un important fournisseur d'armement.

After the war, sporty motorcycles from England became popular in the United States. As a counter, the Milwaukee-based company continued development of the OHV models.

KNUCKLEHEAD

bis zu 160 km/h. Daneben blieben die anspruchslosen Seitenventil-„Flatheads" weiter im Programm. Zu außergewöhnlicher Bekanntheit gelangte die 750er als Militärtyp WLA. 88 000 dieser unzerstörbaren Kradmeldermaschinen zogen in den Zweiten Weltkrieg. Harley-Davidson war zu einem wichtigen Rüstungsbetrieb geworden.

Nach dem Krieg erfreuten sich in den USA sportliche Motorräder aus England großer Beliebtheit. Als Konter entwickelte das in Milwaukee ansässige Unternehmen die ohv-Modelle kontinuierlich weiter.

Après la guerre, les motos sportives anglaises sont très appréciées aux USA. Pour répliquer, l'entreprise de Milwaukee continue sans cesse à faire évoluer ses modèles à soupapes en tête. Le moteur baptisé « panhead » en raison de la forme en poêle de son cache-culbuteur est plus fiable et plus performant que le knucklehead, mais il est aussi plus lourd. Fourche télescopique, bras oscillant sur la roue arrière (à partir de 1958) et accessoires de tourisme transforment peu à peu les grandes Harleys en luxueuses motos de tourisme.

The engine, known as a panhead due to its pan-shaped valve cover, offered more reliability and better performance than the knucklehead but had to lug more weight around. Telescopic forks, rear swinging forks (starting in 1958) and touring accessories transformed the big Harleys into luxury cruisers.

In 1952, the company had another ace up its sleeve to combat the sales success of Triumph, Norton and BSA. The engineers thought up a lightweight two-cylinder bike,

Der aufgrund seiner pfannenförmigen Ventildeckel „Panhead" genannte Motor war zuverlässiger und leistungsfähiger als der Knucklehead, hatte allerdings mehr Gewicht zu schleppen. Telegabel, Hinterradschwinge (ab 1958) und Tourenzubehör verwandelten die großen Harleys zunehmend in luxuriöse Reisedampfer.

En 1952, l'entreprise sort un autre as de sa manche pour répondre aux succès commerciaux de Triumph, Norton et BSA. Les techniciens conçoivent une machine bicylindre légère, le modèle K, qui donna naissance à partir de 1957 à la légendaire Sportster. Son bicylindre en V de 900 cm^3 enthousiasme alors surtout les clients les plus jeunes. Ceux qui privilégient le confort peuvent se tourner à partir de 1966 vers les modèles Shovelhead. Appelées Electra-Glide, ces motos offrent alors un plaisir sans limite aux amateurs de tourisme, avec leurs

PANHEAD

the K model, which evolved into the legendary Sportster in 1957. Its dynamic 900 cc V-Twin was a big hit with younger customers in particular. Those looking for more comfort could opt for the shovelhead models starting in 1966. Under the name Electra Glide, they promised limitless fun on the road—with cases, a windshield and an electric starter. But the 1200 cc engine was also available in an unadorned variant called the Super Glide. It combined the Big Twin chassis with the fork and front wheel from the Sportster family.

1952 zog die Company ein weiteres Ass gegen die Verkaufserfolge von Triumph, Norton und BSA aus dem Ärmel. Die Techniker erdachten eine leichte Zweizylindermaschine – das K-Modell –, aus der ab 1957 die legendäre Sportster wurde. Ihr dynamischer 900-ccm-V-Twin begeisterte vor allem jüngere Kunden. Wer es gemütlicher wollte, der konnte ab 1966 auf die Shovelhead-Modelle zurückgreifen. Als Electra-Glide versprachen sie grenzenlosen Touringspaß – mit Koffern, Windschild und Elektrostarter.

coffres, leur pare-brise et leur démarreur électrique. Mais le moteur de 1 200 cm³ fut aussi utilisé sur une version plus sportive, la Superglide. Cette machine associe le châssis Big-Twin à la fourche et à la roue avant de la gamme Sportster. Dans les années soixante-dix, les puissances des motos japonaises ne cessent de croître, et Harley-Davidson fait passer à 1340 cm³ la cylindrée de son moteur Shovelhead qui avait entre-temps vieilli.

SPORTSTER

Due to the continuous rise in engine performance among Japanese motorcycles in the seventies, Harley-Davidson increased the displacement of the shovelhead engine, which had since become outdated, to 1 340 cc.

Aber der 1200-ccm-Motor bot sich auch für eine pure Variante an, die Super Glide. Bei ihr vereinte sich das Big-Twin-Chassis mit Gabel und Vorderrad der Sportster-Familie. Weil die Motorleistungen bei den japanischen Motorrädern in den Siebzigerjahren stetig anstiegen, erhöhte Harley-Davidson den Hubraum des mittlerweile antiken Shovelhead-Motors auf 1 340 ccm.

Um der japanischen Invasion etwas entgegenzusetzen, kreierten die US-Techniker außerdem in Zusammenarbeit mit dem Porsche-Entwicklungszentrum in Weissach ein völlig neues Aggregat. Anders als seine Vorgänger war der ab 1984 erhältliche 1340-ccm Evolution-Motor vollständig aus Aluminium gefertigt. Trotz aller Innovationen

Pour faire face à l'invasion japonaise, les techniciens américains conçoivent un tout nouveau moteur en collaboration avec le centre de développement Porsche de Weissach. Contrairement à ses prédécesseurs, ce groupe de 1340 cm³ disponible à partir de 1984 est entièrement en aluminium. Malgré toutes ses innovations, il affiche toujours un angle de 45°, comme toute bonne Harley-Davidson classique. Ce moteur fiable a donné naissance à d'innombrables modèles et versions, par exemple les types « Softtail » avec leur ébauche d'arrière à cadre rigide. Pour les modèles Sportster, l'entreprise américaine conçoit en 1986 un moteur Evolution d'une cylindrée de 883 cm³ et 1100 cm³ (1200 cm³ à partir de 1988), chargé de remplacer les anciens Ironhead-Sportster 1000.

In order to offer some opposition to the invasion of Japanese bikes, engineers in the US worked with the Porsche development center in Weissach, Germany to create an entirely new design. Unlike its predecessor, the 1340 cc Evolution engine launched in 1984 was made entirely out of aluminum. Despite all of the innovations, it maintained the 45° cylinder angle associated with classic Harley-Davidson bikes. This reliable engine provided the basis for countless model variants, such as the Softail types with the appearance of a rigid-frame rear-end.

verfügte er über einen Zylinderwinkel von 45° – wie es sich für eine klassische Harley-Davidson gehört. Auf Basis dieses zuverlässigen Triebwerks entstanden unzählige Modellvarianten, etwa die „Softail"-Typen mit angedeutetem Starrrahmenheck. Auch für die Sportster-Modelle ersannen die Amerikaner 1986 einen Evolution-Motor, der mit 883 ccm und zunächst 1100 ccm (ab 1988 dann 1200 ccm) die bisherigen 1000er-Ironhead-Sportster ablöste.

En 2002 Harley Davidson se lance sur un terrain totalement nouveau pour elle lorsqu'elle lance la V-Rod. Équipée d'un moteur « Revolution » à arbres à cames en tête, refroidi par eau et affichant un angle du V de 60°, cette puissante moto de tourisme s'éloigne considérablement des traditionnelles machines américaines.

EVOULUTION

The Americans also devised an Evolution engine for Sportster models in 1986. The engine, starting at 883 cc and then 1100 cc (and then 1200 cc from 1988) replaced the earlier 1000 cc Ironhead Sportster.

In 2002, the company ventured into entirely unknown terrain when it presented its newly developed V-Rod. The high-performance cruiser outfitted with a water-cooled DOHC Revolution engine with 60° cylinder angle reflected only the faintest hints of traditional US bikes. But tradition-focused Harley

Auf ein völlig unbekanntes Parkett begab sich die Company im Modelljahr 2002, als sie die neu entwickelte V-Rod präsentierte. Der mit einem wassergekühlten dohc-Revolution-Triebwerk (double overhead camshaft, 2 × ohc) mit 60°-Zylinderwinkel ausgestattete Power-Cruiser erinnerte nur noch entfernt an die traditionellen US-Bikes. Doch traditionsbewusste Harley-Fahrer mussten sich keine Sorgen machen. Parallel hatten die Amerikaner den Evolution-Motor

Mais les fidèles de la marque n'ont pas de souci à se faire. En parallèle, l'usine continue à développer le moteur Evolution, qui, dans sa version TwinCam, est pour la première fois disponible avec un arbre d'équilibrage pour réduire les vibrations. Avec une cylindrée allant de 1449 à 1802 cm³, le TwinCam devient le moteur standard de tous les modèles Big-Twin, de la Dyna aux grosses machines de tourisme, en passant par la Softail. Sur le moteur « Milwaukee Eight » présenté en 2017, quatre soupapes par cylindre et un refroidissement liquide optionnel des

REVOLUTION

riders did not have to worry. At the same time, the Americans had continued development of the Evolution engine to the Twin Cam, which was also available with a vibration-damping balance shaft. Offering 1449 to 1802 cc, the Twin Cam was the standard engine for all Big Twin models from the Dyna to the Softail to the heavy touring bikes. In the Milwaukee-Eight engine introduced in 2017, four valves per head and optional liquid cooling for the cylinder heads ensure that the latest limits on exhaust and noise emissions can be met. And, at 91 to 102 HP, the driving performance of the big Harley models is reaching levels never seen before.

zum Twin Cam weiterentwickelt, der erstmals auch mit vibrationshemmender Ausgleichswelle erhältlich war.

Mit 1449 bis 1802 ccm war der Twin Cam der Standardmotor für alle Big-Twin-Modelle von Dyna über Softail bis zu den schweren Tourern. Beim 2017 eingeführten „Milwaukee Eight"-Motor sorgen Vierventilköpfe und eine optionale Flüssigkeitskühlung der Zylinderköpfe dafür, dass aktuelle Abgas- und Geräuschgrenzwerte eingehalten werden können. Und mit 91 bis 102 PS erreichen die Fahrleistungen der großen Harley-Modelle bislang völlig unbekannte Dimensionen.

TWIN CAM

culasses permettent de respecter les normes d'échappement et de bruit. Et avec des puissances allant de 91 à 102 ch, les performances des grandes Harley atteignent des niveaux encore totalement inédits.

ADVERTISING

Soon after the founding of Harley-Davidson Motor Co., its management recognized the positive effects of advertising. Graphics designed with exacting detail presented tales of perfect riding comfort, high reliability and success in motorsports. Oftentimes the advertisements focused on conveying a certain attitude towards life. This is precisely how the ads worked, starting in the fifties. If you can believe the ads, riders of Harley-Davidson motorcycles are happy and successful. And maybe there's really something to that after all.

Other products that have little to do with motorcycles are happy to capitalize on the cool image of the Harley-Davidson brand – cigarettes, clothing and alcoholic beverages. A Harley now provides the ideal means of succinctly conveying a lifestyle of freedom and adventure.

Schon bald nach der Gründung der Harley-Davidson Motor Co. erkannte die Geschäftsführung den positiven Effekt von Werbeanzeigen. Aufwendig gestaltete Grafiken erzählten von perfektem Reisekomfort, hoher Zuverlässigkeit und Erfolgen beim Sport. Oft ging es auch nur darum, ein bestimmtes Lebensgefühl zu vermitteln. Genau das ist es, was die Anzeigen ab den Fünfzigerjahren ausmachte. Glaubt man ihnen, dann sind Fahrer einer Harley-Davidson glücklich und erfolgreich. Und wer weiß, vielleicht ist da ja sogar etwas dran.

Gerne schmücken sich auch andere Produkte, die kaum etwas mit Motorrädern zu tun haben, mit dem coolen Image der Marke Harley-Davidson – Zigaretten, Bekleidung oder alkoholische Getränke. Eine Harley transportiert nun einmal auf ideale Weise den Lifestyle von Freiheit und Abenteuer.

Très vite après la création de Harley-Davidson Motor Co., les dirigeants prennent conscience de l'effet positif des annonces publicitaires. Des graphismes très élaborés évoquent le confort de voyage, le haut niveau de fiabilité, les succès sportifs. À l'époque, le but est d'évoquer le bonheur de vivre. C'est ce qui fait la particularité des publicités des années cinquante. Si on suit le message, les conducteurs de Harley-Davidson sont des gens qui réussissent dans la vie et sont heureux. Et qui sait, peut-être qu'il y a du vrai...

Et puis d'autres produits très éloignés de la moto chercheront à récupérer l'image tendance de la marque Harley-Davidson : cigarettes, vêtements, boissons alcooliques. Harley est un vecteur idéal pour faire passer l'idée d'un mode de vie marqué par la liberté et l'aventure.

NEW

Brilliant and

Beautiful

The Enthusiast

A MAGAZINE FOR MOTORCYCLISTS

SEPTEMBER 1942

MOTORCYCLING
THE GREATEST SPORT OF THEM ALL!

1931
HARLEY-DAVIDSON

Enjoy Motorcycling More

With

HARLEY-DAVIDSON ACCESSORIES

Everything for the Motorcyclist
APPROVED MOTORCYCLE ACCESSORIES
for 1940

IF YOUR DEALER CANNOT SUPPLY YOU . . . WRITE DIRECT TO

HARLEY - DAVIDSON MOTOR CO.

MILWAUKEE, WISCONSIN, U.S.A.
IN U.S. DOLLARS F. O. B. MILWAUKEE, WIS., U. S. A. ALL DUTIES, TAXES, TRANSPORTATION, EXTRA.
QUOTED SUBJECT TO CHANGE WITHOUT NOTICE

HARLEY-DAVIDSON
announcement
news bulletin

1955
Models

NUMBER 1204 . . . AUGUST 9, 1954

OVERWHELMING EMOTIONS. AND GOOSE-BUMPS EVERY TIME.

Brake as late as possible. Stay on the outside. Hit the apex of the curve. Accelerate. Brake. Lean in. Keep going. Faster. Stay on the bike. Hit the apex. Accelerate. Stay on the bike. Wipe-outs hurt. They brutalize your body and your bike. They ruin your chances. Stay on the bike. And fight. Every lap, every turn, every second. Fight to the end. Fight to the top. The goosebumps never go away.

GROSSE EMOTIONEN. UND IMMER WIEDER DIESE GÄNSEHAUT.

Bremse so spät wie möglich. Bleibe außen. Triff den Apex, den Scheitelpunkt der Kurve. Beschleunige. Bremse. Lege dich nach innen. Noch weiter. Noch schneller. Bleibe auf dem Motorrad. Triff den Apex. Beschleunige. Bleibe auf dem Motorrad. Stürze tun weh. Sie schaden deinem Körper und deinem Bike. Sie machen deine Chancen zunichte. Bleibe auf dem Motorrad. Und kämpfe. Jede Runde, jede Kurve, jede Sekunde. Kämpfe bis zum Ende. Kämpfe dich ganz nach oben. Die Gänsehaut, sie bleibt.

GRANDES ÉMOTIONS. ET TOUJOURS CETTE CHAIR DE POULE.

Freine le plus tard possible. Reste à l'extérieur. Fais attention au point de corde. Accélère. Freine. Penche-toi vers l'intérieur. Encore. Encore plus vite. Reste sur la moto. Prends le point de corde. Accélère. Reste sur la moto. Les chutes font mal. Elles abîment ton corps et ta machine. Elles réduisent tes chances à néant. Reste sur la moto. Et lutte. À chaque tour, à chaque virage, à chaque seconde. Lutte jusqu'au bout. Lutte pour aller le plus haut possible. La chair de poule, elle ne te quitte pas.

DRIVE, DRIFT, FLAT TRACK

PHOTOS: HARLEY-DAVIDSON

Nothing could be more manly than flat track racing. Riders race around tracks in groups without fear in non-stop competitions and drift around sandy turns. The riders rely entirely on their own skills, sturdy bikes and the fact that risky maneuvers are just an everyday part of this extreme motorsport. Flat track racing is an awesome spectacle that keeps riders close to the ground, with plenty of action and charged emotions.

Flat-Track-Piloten sind ganze Kerle. Sie stechen im Geschwader sorgenfrei, ungebremst und schräg driftend in sandige Kurven. Die Fahrer vertrauen dabei allein auf ihr Können, urwüchsige Maschinen und den Umstand, dass grenzgängerische Manöver einfach zum Alltag dieses radikalen Motorsports gehören. Flat Track Racing ist ein verdammt erdverbundenes Spektakel – mit viel Action und großen Emotionen.

Les pilotes de flat track sont de vrais durs. À la lutte en peloton, ils ne s'inquiètent de rien, en glissade sans freins dans les virages de sable. Ils ne se fient qu'à leur savoir-faire et à leurs machines brutales, conscients du fait que les manœuvres à la limite font partie du quotidien de ce sport mécanique extrême. Les courses de flat track, c'est du combat au ras du sol, c'est beaucoup d'action et des émotions fortes.

In the 1920s, this success story began with a massive movement in the USA. The development of faster bikes resulted in sand tracks in all corners of the country almost overnight. Courses made of solid wood or concrete were often inaccessible. Harleys with manual transmissions became the best weapons on the clay surface of flat tracks. Now, the XG 750 R is reintroducing this impressive legacy to the modern era.

In den 1920er-Jahren, mit der Massenmobilisierung in den USA, begann diese Erfolgsgeschichte. Dank immer schnellerer Maschinen entstanden quasi über Nacht Sandbahnen in allen Ecken des Landes. Feste Pisten aus Holz oder Beton waren oft unerreichbar. Handgeschaltete Harleys entwickelten sich zur schärfsten Waffe auf dem lehmigen Boden der Flat Tracks. Heute trägt die XG 750 R dieses große Erbe in die Neuzeit.

Cette réussite commence dans les années vingt, avec la mobilisation de masse aux USA. Les machines devenant de plus en plus rapides, les pistes de sable apparaissent presque du jour au lendemain dans tous les coins du pays. Les pistes en dur, en bois ou en béton, sont souvent irréalisables. Les Harleys à boîte manuelle s'avèrent vite être l'arme la plus affûtée sur le sol glaiseux des flat tracks. Aujourd'hui, la XG 750 R est l'héritière de plein de droit de cette grande époque.

PHOTOS: DA GURU PHOTOGRAPHY

HIGHWAY TO HORIZO

The key to success in drag racing is a perfect alliance of human and machine. To win the quarter-mile, you shake, rattle and roll the bike to its limit with a white-knuckle grip – and are fully in the zone when the green lights hit. This helps the burnout slick to achieve maximum traction with the ground and the long bike accelerates towards the finish line in no time thanks to a finely tared clutch and a long wheelie bar. Straight ahead into the distance.

Der Schlüssel zum Erfolg beim Drag Racing liegt in der perfekten Symbiose aus Mensch und Maschine. Denn die Viertelmeile besiegt nur, wer das kreischende Material bis zum Limit reizt, die Sehnen spannt und beim Erlöschen der Startampel – Christmas Tree genannt – ganz bei sich ist. Nur dann stemmt sich der vom Burnout aufgeheizte Slick optimal in den Boden und peitscht die lange Maschine, dank perfekt tarierter Kupplung und einer langen Wheelie Bar, in wenigen Augenblicken gen Horizont. Geradewegs ins Jenseits.

Dans les courses de dragsters, la clé de la réussite réside dans la symbiose parfaite entre l'homme et la machine. Car pour vaincre sur le quart de mile, il faut tirer sur le matériel jusqu'à la limite, tendre les muscles et être totalement concentré au moment où s'éteignent les feux de l'« arbre de Noël ». Chauffée à bloc, la gomme du pneu slick adhère au maximum au sol et en quelques instants, grâce à un embrayage calibré avec une précision maximale et au long guidon, propulse la longue machine vers l'horizon... quasiment dans l'au-delà.

s in the USA, amateur racers once
or supremacy on DIY-modified
r Twins on a 402-meter long asphalt
w, the sport is a major event. Pro
ss V-Rods with a 2.6-liter engine
accelerate to speeds exceeding
h in less than seven seconds. The
ds, muscular as a bicep, make an in-
oise that is music to the ears of
European fans. Spectators in the
urrounding the drag strips go crazy
ull throttle show featuring the two-
eedsters.

Bei den Sprints in den USA quälten sich
einst Hobby-Racer mit hausgemachten
Sportster-Twins über die 402,34 Meter lange
Teerbahn. Heute ist der Sport ein riesiges
Happening, bei dem V-Rods der Pro-Stock-
Klasse mit 2,6 Litern Hubraum in weniger
als sieben Sekunden auf über 300 km/h
beschleunigen. Doch auch in Europa klingt
der infernalische Lärm aus oberarmdicken
Krümmern wie eine Sinfonie in den Ohren
jubelnder Fans. Auf den Rängen der Dragstrips liebt man die irre Vollgas-Show mit
den zweirädrigen Kanonenkugeln.

À une époque révolue, les sprints orga
aux USA réunissaient des amateurs q
raient leurs Sportster-Twins bricolées
402 mètres d'asphalte. Aujourd'hui, c
est devenu quelque chose de gigantes
avec des V-Rods de classe Pro-Stock, é
de moteurs de 2,6 litres de cylindrée c
passer les machines à plus de 300 km
moins de sept secondes. Mais en Euro
si, le bruit infernal des collecteurs gr
comme l'avant-bras sonne comme un
phonie aux oreilles des fans enthousi
Dans les tribunes des dragstrips, on a
spectacle dingue de boulets de canon

SALT AND PEPPER

PHOTOS: ALEXANDER BABIC

The passionate, unquenchable desire for speed still inspires enthusiasts such as customizer Shinya Kimura. Stretched out over the low iron of the bike, with the wavering horizon in sight, every rider can redefine his or her limits. This enthralling game with the forces of nature began 100 years ago on dried-out salt flats and flat beaches.

Von der nicht enden wollenden Sehnsucht nach Geschwindigkeit werden Enthusiasten wie Customizer Shinya Kimura bis heute inspiriert. Denn lang über das flache Eisen gestreckt, den Horizont fest im Blick, kann jeder Fahrer seine Grenzen neu definieren. Ein reizvolles Spiel mit den Naturgewalten, das vor 100 Jahren auf ausgetrockneten Salt Flats und flachen Stränden seinen Anfang nahm.

Aujourd'hui encore, les passionnés comme le transformateur Shinya Kimura sont inspirés par une recherche sans fin de vitesse. Couchés à plat, le regard fixé sur l'horizon tremblotant, chaque pilote peut redéfinir ses propres limites. Un jeu séduisant avec les forces de la nature a vu le jour il y a 100 ans sur des lacs salés séchés et de grandes plages plates.

55

When the Harley plant first attempted to break the speed record in 1937, Joe Petrali and the Knucklehead engine were unstoppable. The covered Twin raced across Daytona Beach at 219 km/h. This world record was unbroken for eleven years straight.

It wasn't until 1965 that the Milwaukee-based company earned a new title on the Bonneville Salt Flats. Sports legend George Roeder accelerated to 285 km/h on a Harley 250 streamliner motorcycle. Five years later, Cal Rayborn managed to reach speeds of 426 km/h on Denis Manning's streamliner and a Sportster engine in tow. Though the rider in the streamliner motorcycle could not see the road surface, this did not make too much of a difference.

Als das Harley-Werk 1937 erstmals zum Angriff auf den Geschwindigkeitsrekord blies, führte kein Weg an Joe Petrali und dem Knucklehead-Motor vorbei. Der verkleidete Twin raste mit 219 km/h über den Strand von Daytona. Ein Weltrekord, der volle elf Jahre Bestand haben sollte.

Erst 1965 gelang es, auf dem Salz von Bonneville einen neuen Titel nach Milwaukee zu holen. Sportlegende George Roeder pilotierte eine verkleidete 250er auf 285 Sachen. Cal Rayborn brachte es fünf Jahre später in Denis Mannings Streamliner – mit dem Vorderrad zwischen den Beinen und einem Sportster-Motor im Gepäck – sogar auf sagenhafte 426 km/h. Dass der Fahrer in der Zigarre die Fahrbahn nicht sah, störte nur am Rande.

Lorsqu'en 1937, l'usine Harley s'attaque pour la première fois au record de vitesse, elle n'a pas d'autre choix que de faire appel au duo composé de Joe Petrali et du moteur knucklehead. La Twin carénée file à 219 km/h sur la plage de Daytona. Un record mondial qui tiendra quand même onze ans.

Il faudra attendre 1965 et le lac salé de Bonneville pour ramener un nouveau titre à Milwaukee. Le légendaire George Roeder pilote alors une 250 carénée qu'il amène à 285 à l'heure. Cinq ans plus tard, Cal Rayborn atteignit la fabuleuse vitesse de 426 km/h sur le streamliner de Denis Manning, la roue avant entre les jambes et un moteur de Sportster à l'arrière. Le fait que le pilote enfermé dans le cigare ne puisse pas voir la piste n'a quasiment dérangé personne.

BURN THE
RICEBURNERS DOWN!

It must have been about two in the morning. A hellish
noise jolted me out of my sleep. It was like a Boeing 747
was lifting off right from my pillow. The others joined me
as we crawled out of our tents to witness a bizarre ritual.
A massive jet of flame was shooting out of a giant machine to set fire to a whole stack of motorcycles. And not
just any motorcycles. There in Sturgis we were witness-
ing the traditional burning of Japanese bikes. They did it
as a sort of ritual against the "rice burners" (a pejorative
term for Japanese bikes). They were not welcome at the
classic "Harley's only!" rallies. Neither here in Sturgis nor
anywhere else.

Es muss gegen zwei Uhr nachts gewesen sein. Höllischer
Lärm riss mich aus dem Schlaf. Mindestens so laut, als
wenn direkt unter deinem Kopfkissen eine Boeing 747
abhebt. Mit mir krochen auch andere aus ihren Zelten.
Und wurden Zeugen eines bizarren Rituals: Ein mächtiger
Feuerstrahl, der aus einer riesigen Maschine schoss,
setzte zu einem Stapel geschichtete Motorräder in Brand.
Nicht irgendwelche Motorräder. Was sich da in Sturgis
abspielte, war das traditionelle Verbrennen japanischer
Bikes: ein bisschen Voodoo gegen die „rice burners", wie
diese ein wenig despektierlich genannt werden. Die haben
auf den klassischen „Harleys only!"-Treffen auch nichts
verloren. Weder hier in Sturgis noch anderswo.

Il devait être deux heures du matin. Un bruit d'enfer m'ar-
rache du sommeil. C'est au minimum comme si un Boeing
747 était en train de décoller directement sous mon oreiller.
Comme les autres, je rampe hors de ma tente. Nous
sommes témoins d'un rituel bizarre : sorti d'une gigantesque machine, un puissant jet de feu enflamme un tas
de motos empilées. Pas n'importe quelles motos. Ce qui se
passe à Sturgis cette nuit-là, c'est le traditionnel incendie
de machines japonaises : un peu de vaudou pour ces
motos qui « carburent au riz », comme on dit ici avec un
manque de respect certain. Après tout, elles n'ont rien à
faire dans une réunion réservée aux Harleys classiques.
Ni ici à Sturgis, ni ailleurs.

EUROPEAN BIKE WEEK
LAKE FAAK, AUSTRIA

PHOTOS: HARLEY-DAVIDSON

For ten days, the ground quakes around Lake Faak in the Austrian state of Carinthia—an otherwise idyllic locale. The heartbeat of Harley-Davidson can be felt throughout the Austrian Alps during European Bike Week, a recurring event where more than 100,000 Harley and custom bike riders gather together. Fans of American bikes travel from all over Europe to celebrate the spirit of the brand.

Zehn Tage lang bebt die Erde am sonst so idyllischen Faaker See in Kärnten. Immer dann, wenn sich über 100 000 Harley- und Custombike-Fahrer zur European Bike Week zusammenfinden, schlägt das Herz von Harley-Davidson in den österreichischen Alpen. Aus ganz Europa kommen US-Bike-Freunde angereist, um den Spirit der Marke zu feiern.

Pendant dix jours, la terre tremble sur les bords du lac d'ordinaire si tranquille de Faak, dans la région autrichienne de Carynthie. À chaque fois que plus de 100 000 conducteurs de Harley et de machines personnalisées se réunissent à l'occasion de cette semaine européenne de la moto, le cœur de Harley-Davidson bat dans les Alpes autrichiennes. Les amateurs de motos américaines de toute l'Europe s'y retrouvent pour célébrer l'esprit de la marque.

Shortly after its founding in 1998, "Faak" grew into Europe's largest event in the Harley-Davidson and biker scene and the third-largest motorcycle rally in the world.

The ring road circles around the turquoise-blue mountain lake to provide access to numerous villages and becomes a high-traffic one-way street for the duration of Bike Week. Ride-in bike shows, rock concerts and stunt demonstrations draw huge crowds and create the show area that forms the center of the impressive event.

Schon kurz nach seiner Gründung im Jahr 1998 wuchs „Faak" zur größten Veranstaltung der Harley-Davidson- und Biker-Szene Europas und zum drittgrößten Motorradtreffen weltweit an.

Über die Ringstraße rund um den türkisblauen Bergsee, die während der Bike Week zur viel befahrenen Einbahnstraße wird, können die diversen Villages erreicht werden. Mit Ride-in-Bikeshows, Rockkonzerten oder Stuntvorführungen bilden diese Show-Areas das Herzstück des imposanten Events.

Très vite après sa création en 1998, « Faak » est devenu la plus grande manifestation européenne de la communauté Harley-Davidson et le troisième plus grand rassemblement de motards du monde.

La route circulaire qui entoure les eaux turquoise du lac de montagne se transforme pendant une semaine en voie à sens unique permettant de se rendre dans les différents « villages ». Proposant des ride-in-bikeshows, des concerts de rock et des démonstrations de cascades, ces zones de spectacle constituent le centre de cette immense manifestation.

The villages also serve as the prime location for individual custom bike makers to set up booths to showcase their latest motorcycle creations. Once visitors have experienced enough hustle and bustle, they can set out on challenging tours through the nearby Alpine landscape. The annual highlight takes place on Saturday, where 25,000 riders set out together on a Harley ride around Lake Faak.

Die Villages sind auch erste Adresse für internationale Customizer, die an eigenen Ständen ihre neuesten Bike-Kreationen präsentieren. Wer genug vom Trubel hat, der kann anspruchsvolle Touren durch die nahe gelegene Berglandschaft unternehmen. Beim jährlichen Highlight, der Harley-Parade rund um den Faaker See, unternehmen bis zu 25 000 Motorradfahrer am Samstagmittag eine gemeinsame Ausfahrt der Superlative.

Les « villages » sont aussi une destination recherchée pour les transformateurs internationaux qui présentent leurs dernières créations sur leurs stands. Ceux que le bruit finit par fatiguer peuvent se lancer dans de belles sorties sur les routes de montagne proches. Lors du clou annuel, la parade des Harleys qui a lieu le samedi à midi autour du lac de Faak, 25 000 motards roulent de concert.

STURGIS
MOTORCYCLE RALLY
USA

PHOTOS: HARLEY-DAVIDSON

It's hot in South Dakota. Very hot. But riding out to the Black Hills in the first week of August is a matter of honor for more than 500,000 people who attend the Sturgis Motorcycle Rally. They come from Minnesota, from New York, from California and even from Europe. Full dressers and baggers are the hot ticket in Sturgis, if only because of the enormous distances that have to be covered.

Es ist heiß in South Dakota. Sehr heiß. Für die über 500 000 Besucher der Sturgis Motorcycle Rally ist es dennoch „Ehrensache", sich in der ersten Augustwoche auf den Weg in die Black Hills zu machen. Sie kommen aus Minnesota, aus New York, aus Kalifornien und auch aus Europa. Full Dresser und Bagger sind das ganz große Ding in Sturgis, schon wegen der gigantischen Entfernungen, die hier zurückgelegt werden müssen.

Il fait chaud dans le Dakota du Sud. Très chaud. Mais pour les plus de 500 000 visiteurs du rallye moto Sturgis, c'est une affaire d'honneur que de se rendre dans les Black Hills durant la première semaine d'août. Ils viennent du Minnesota, de New York, de Californie et même d'Europe. Les machines de grand tourisme, telles les full dressers et baggers, sont de mise à Sturgis, rien que du fait des distances gigantesques à parcourir pour arriver ici.

But sportsters, choppers, bobbers and vintage bikes also find their way to the Sturgis Motorcycle Rally. And most of them have been made by Harley-Davidson in Milwaukee.

Mount Rushmore National Park, with its stony portraits of four former US presidents, is just over 50 miles away and tantalizes many visitors to take a joyride out into the surrounding area. Riders can journey to the nearby states of North Dakota, Wyoming or Montana along picture-perfect mountain roads.

Aber auch Sportster, Chopper, Bobber und Vintage Bikes finden den Weg zur Sturgis Motorcycle Rally. Und die meisten von ihnen wurden bei Harley-Davidson in Milwaukee gefertigt.

Das Mount Rushmore National Memorial mit seinen steinernen Porträts von vier ehemaligen US-Präsidenten ist kaum 50 Meilen entfernt und lockt viele Besucher zu einer Spritztour ins Umland. Die Bundesstaaten North Dakota, Wyoming oder Montana können über malerische Bergstraßen angefahren werden.

Mais les Sportster, Chopper, Bobber et Vintage Bikes sont aussi représentées. La plupart d'entre elles sortent des usines Harley-Davidson du Milwaukee.

Avec ses portraits sculptés de quatre anciens présidents américains, le parc national du mont Rushmore est à moins de 50 miles de là et incite de nombreux visiteurs à faire un détour dans le voisinage. Les États du Dakota du Nord, du Wyoming ou du Montana sont également des destinations proches, que l'on atteint par des routes de montagne pittoresques.

In downtown Sturgis, accessory dealers, bike builders and motorcycle manufacturers use Lazelle Street as a stage for presenting their products for the new season. Dozens of event locations, such as the Buffalo Chip, the Loud American Roadhouse and Full Throttle Saloon, are spread over a wide area and offer rock concerts, bike shows and motorcycle races. And cold beer to quench the scorching heat.

In Downtown Sturgis nutzen Zubehörhändler, Bike Builder und Motorradhersteller die Lazelle Street als Showbühne zur Präsentation ihrer Produkte für die neue Saison. Dutzende über ein weites Areal verteilte Veranstaltungsorte wie Buffalo Chip, The Loud American Roadhouse oder der Full Throttle Saloon bieten Rockkonzerte, Bikeshows und Motorradrennen. Und kühles Bier gegen die sengende Hitze.

Dans la ville de Sturgis, des vendeurs d'accessoires, les petits et grands fabricants de motos se servent de la Lazelle Street comme terrain d'exposition pour présenter leurs nouveaux produits. Éparpillés sur une vaste zone, des dizaines de sites tels que Buffalo Chip, The Loud American Roadhouse ou le Full Throttle Saloon proposent concerts de rock, bikeshows et courses de motos. Sans oublier la bière fraîche, pour résister à la chaleur torride.

DAYTONA BIKE WEEK
USA

PHOTOS: HARLEY-DAVIDSON

In Daytona Beach, motorcycle season gets started early in the middle of March. Hundreds of proud bikers riding down the main drag in an endless stream to show off their modded Harleys to appreciative onlookers can mean only one thing: bike week is back. Rivers of Budweiser flow in the bars on either side of the major streets while one of the world's most famous motorcycle beauty contests is held on Beach Street: The Rats Hole Custom Bike Show.

In Daytona Beach beginnt die Motorradsaison bereits Mitte März. Wenn auf der Main Street Hunderte stolzer Biker pausenlos auf und ab fahren, um den interessierten Passanten ihre umgebauten Harleys zu präsentieren, dann ist wieder Bike Week. In den Saloons rechts und links der Hauptstraßen fließt das Bud in Strömen, während zeitgleich an der Beach Street einer der weltweit bekanntesten Schönheitswettbewerbe für Motorräder abgehalten wird: die Rat's Hole

À Daytona Beach, la saison de moto commence mi-mars. Lorsque sur la Mainstreet, des centaines de fiers motards passent et repassent sans arrêt pour exhiber leurs Harleys transformées aux passants reconnaissants, c'est le retour de la Bike Week. Dans les saloons à droite et à gauche des rues principales, la Bud coule à flot tandis que sur la Beach Street a lieu un des concours de beauté pour motos les plus connus du monde : le Rats Hole Custom

But downtown isn't the only place teeming with motorcycles for ten whole days. Countless bars and show areas far and wide, such as the Iron Horse, Jackson Hole Saloon and Last Resort, also draw in visitors with music and bike contests and entice riders to take relaxing rides between the Atlantic Coast and the Gulf of Mexico.

Doch nicht nur im Stadtzentrum wimmelt es ganze zehn Tage lang nur so vor Motorrädern. Auch weit außerhalb, etwa am Iron Horse Saloon, am Jackson Hole Saloon oder am Last Resort, locken unzählige Bars und Show-Areas mit Musik oder Bike-Contests und verleiten zu entspannten Ausfahrten zwischen Atlantik und Golf von Mexiko.

Pendant dix jours, ça grouille de motos, et pas seulement dans le centre-ville. À l'extérieur, comme sur le Iron Horse, le Jackson Hole Saloon ou le Last Resort, d'innombrables bars et aires de spectacle rivalisent pour attirer les visiteurs avec leurs concours de motos et invitent à des sorties détendues entre l'Atlantique et le

Daytona Bike Week has been held in the sunshine state of Florida since 1937. It all started with races at the Daytona Speedway. The races still take place, but the raucous party pushes them to the sideline more and more every year. Today the famous event draws up to 500,000 visitors and is one of the most well-known and largest motorcycle rallies in the world.

Seit 1937 findet die Daytona Bike Week jährlich im Sunshine State Florida statt. Angefangen hat alles mit Rennen auf dem Daytona Speedway. Die Races finden noch immer statt, sind aber vor lauter Party mehr und mehr in den Hintergrund geraten. Heute zählt die berühmte Veranstaltung mit mehr als 500 000 Besuchern zu den bekanntesten und größten Motorradtreffen der Welt.

Depuis 1937, la Daytona Bike Week a lieu une fois par dans l'État ensoleillé de Floride. Tout a commencé par les courses du circuit de Daytona. Les compétitions ont toujours lieu, mais sont peu à peu passées au second plan derrière la fête. Aujourd'hui, ce célèbre rassemblement regroupe jusqu'à 500 000 visiteurs et fait partie des rassemblements de motards les plus connus et les plus grands du monde.

EVENTS MADE BY HARLEY-DAVIDSON
HAMBURG AND MALLORCA

PHOTOS: HARLEY-DAVIDSON

Harley-Davidson is more than just a motorcycle brand. Harley-Davidson embodies an attitude towards life that is best shared with like-minded people. As a result, the company hosts its own events throughout Europe—with bike shows, stretches of showcases and rock concerts—and gathers the Harley community at popular hotspots.

Harley-Davidson ist nicht nur eine Motorradmarke. Harley-Davidson verkörpert ein Lebensgefühl, das sich am besten mit Gleichgesinnten teilen lässt. Folglich veranstaltet die Company eigene Events in ganz Europa mit Bikeshows, Shoppingmeilen und Rockkonzerten und trommelt die Harley-Gemeinde zu den angesagten Hotspots zusammen.

Harley-Davidson n'est pas qu'une marque de moto. Harley-Davidson incarne un état d'esprit, une conception de la vie qu'on a forcément envie de partager avec d'autres. C'est pour cela que l'entreprise organise ses propres manifestations dans toute l'Europe, avec des bikeshows, des expositions de vente et des concerts de rock, et lance des appels à la communauté pour qu'elle se retrouve sur les sites annoncés.

Both Harley Dome Cologne held along a kilometer-long downtown stretch in the Deutz neighborhood of Cologne and Hamburg Harley Days offer some urban flair. Three event locations at Hamburg's Großmarkt grounds, the legendary Reeperbahn district and the downtown area draw in 500,000 visitors to the city on the Elbe every year. The European H.O.G. Rally heads for new destinations in Europe every year, while the Harley-Davidson Euro Festival has found its home on the Bay of Saint-Tropez.

But Harley-Davidson is not the only company capable of organizing great rallies. The scene started creating its own rollicking events long ago, including the Harley-Davidson Summertime Party on the North Sea island of Sylt, Magic Bike at Rüdesheim in western Germany with its fantastic stretches of road in the Middle Rhine Valley, and Mallorca Bike Week at Robinson Club Cala Serena in late fall.

Urbanes Flair bieten sowohl Harley Dome Cologne auf einem citynahen, einen Kilometer langen Areal in Köln-Deutz als auch die Hamburg Harley Days. Gleich drei Event-Locations auf dem Hamburger Großmarkt, der legendären Reeperbahn und der Mönckebergstraße locken alljährlich bis zu 500 000 Besucher an die Elbe. Die European H.O.G. Rally steuert jedes Jahr neue Ziele innerhalb Europas an, während das Harley-Davidson Euro Festival seine Heimat am Golf von Saint-Tropez gefunden hat.

Doch nicht nur Harley-Davidson ist in der Lage, großartige Veranstaltungen zu organisieren. Längst sorgt die Szene selbst für ausgelassene Events, sei es bei der Harley-Davidson Summertime Party auf der Nordseeinsel Sylt, der Magic Bike in Rüdesheim mit traumhaften Strecken im Mittelrheintal oder im Spätherbst auf der Mallorca Bike Week im Robinson Club Cala Serena.

Dans le style urbain, citons le « Harley Dome Cologne » qui se tient sur une zone d'un kilomètre proche du centre-ville, à Cologne-Deutz, et les Hamburg Harley Days. Le rassemblement de Hambourg est réparti sur trois sites : les halles centrales de Hambourg, la légendaire Reeperbahn et le centre-ville, et il attire chaque année 500 000 visiteurs sur les bords de l'Elbe. Le European H.O.G. Rally a lieu chaque année à des endroits différents, tandis que le Harley-Davidson Euro Festival s'est installé à demeure sur les bords du golfe de Saint-Tropez.

Mais Harley-Davidson n'est pas seul à organiser de grandes manifestations. Depuis longtemps, la communauté se prend elle-même en charge à l'occasion de rassemblements débridés, qu'il s'agisse de la Harley-Davidson Summertime Party, qui a lieu à Sylt, une île allemande de la mer du Nord, de la Magic Bike, qui se tient à Rüdesheim et offre de merveilleux circuits dans la vallée du Rhin moyen, ou de la Mallorca Bike Week, organisée à la fin de l'automne au Robinson Club Cala Serena.

"WHERE'S YOUR WILL TO BE WEIRD?"
(JIM MORRISON)

The desire for individuality—the desire to be different—is the essential driving force behind altering a stock motorcycle, i.e. customizing. That's how it was in the early '60s. In California, people were modifying old Knuckleheads and not-so-old Panheads to create bikes in the West Coast style. The most famous motorcycle in the world, Captain America from the movie "Easy Rider" is one example. It was based on a worn-out police vehicle that allowed for almost all of the parts to be lopped off. Once you take most of the parts away, you're left with little more than an elegant engine in one fine-looking frame. And a sound you cannot find anywhere else. To this day, the 45° twin-engine bikes from Milwaukee have been providing the foundation for almost everything that can be called a genuine chopper. Or a bobber. Or a flat tracker. Or a …

Der Wunsch nach Individualität, nach dem Anderssein, ist essenzielle Triebfeder für die Umgestaltung eines Serien-motorrads, für das Customizing. So war es schon in den frühen Sechzigern, als in Kalifornien aus alten Knuckle-heads und nicht ganz so alten Panheads die typischen West Coast Styler entstanden. Wie beispielsweise das berühmtes-te Motorrad der Welt, „Captain America" aus „Easy Rider", basierend auf einem ausgedienten Polizeifahrzeug, das sich einfach und radikal choppen, also abhacken, lässt. Nach dem Cutdown bleibt nicht viel mehr übrig als ein form-schöner Motor in einem ästhetischen Rahmen. Und so ist es bis heute: Die 45-Grad-Twins aus Milwaukee sind Basis für fast alles, was einmal ein waschechter Chopper werden soll. Oder Bobber. Oder Flat Tracker. Oder …

La recherche de personnalisation, de différence, est une des motivations essentielles de transformation de motos de série. C'est ainsi que sont nées au début des années soixante, en Californie, les westcoast-stylers typiques, réalisées à partir de Knuckleheads anciennes ou de Panheads plus récentes. Par exemple la moto plus célèbre du monde, la « Captain America » du film « Easy Rider », basée sur une moto de police réformée, transformée de manière simple et radicale, « choppée » comme on dit là-bas. Après la découpe, il ne reste pas grand-chose d'autre qu'un beau moteur dans un cadre esthétique. Et puis ce son unique. Jusqu'à aujourd'hui, les twins à 45° de Milwaukee sont à la base de presque tous les authen-tiques choppers. Ou des bobbers. Ou bien des flat trackers. Ou encore…

ONE WAY MACHINE
SINGAPORE SUN AND IRON RIOT

Like father, like son. This rule doesn't always apply. But in the case of Julian von Oheimb and his father Claudius, there is a kernel of truth in this cliche. Without the example set by his father, who rode Knuckles, Flats and Pans through the Middle German prairie, his life certainly would have turned out differently. Julian is now an engineer, metal artist, designer and the mastermind of One Way Machine, one of the most trendy labels for classic custom Harleys.

Wie der Vater, so der Sohn. Nicht immer trifft diese Regel zu. Im Falle von Julian von Oheimb und seinem Vater Claudius liegt im fragwürdigen Klischee aber durchaus ein Funken Wahrheit. Denn ohne die Prägung seines Vorbilds, das schon vor Jahrzehnten Knuckles, Flats und Pans durch die mittelhessische Prärie trieb, wäre es sicher anders gekommen. Heute ist Julian Ingenieur, Metallkünstler, Designer und Mastermind von One Way Machine, einem der angesagtesten Labels für zeitlose Custom-Harleys.

Tel père, tel fils. Une règle qui ne se vérifie pas toujours. Mais dans le cas de Julian von Oheimb et de son père Claudius, ce cliché douteux recèle certainement un fond de vérité. Car s'il n'avait pas été marqué par son modèle qui sillonnait il y a plusieurs décennies les terrains du centre de l'Allemagne sur des knuckles, des flats et des pans, les choses auraient sûrement été différentes. Aujourd'hui, Julian est ingénieur, artiste du métal, designer et maître d'œuvre de One Way Machine, un des labels les plus réputés en matière de personnalisation de Harleys.

SINGAPORE SUN - The "Singapore Sun" got off to a rocky start. It was made worse in Asia with the addition of tires that were too wide and a long fork. Then, One Way Machine stepped in to give them a second wind. Julian adjusted the chassis with lugged tires and a hill-climbing fork. He poured plenty of black paint over the old Triumph tank and hand-crafted mounted parts, which provides a perfect contrast to the accents from the shining brass. The proud owner in Singapore knows that this show bike is great to ride.

SINGAPORE SUN - Die Singapore Sun hatte einen schweren Start. Mit viel zu breiten Reifen und langer Gabel wurde sie in Asien verschlimmbessert, bevor ihr One Way Machine neues Leben einhauchte. Julian rückte das Fahrwerk mit Stollenreifen und einer Hillclimb-Gabel zurecht. Über den alten Triumph-Tank und handgefertigte Anbauteile goss er reichlich schwarze Farbe, was perfekt mit den Akzenten aus schimmerndem Messing kontrastiert. Der stolze Besitzer in Singapur weiß zu schätzen, dass man dieses Show-Bike wirklich fahren kann.

SINGAPORE SUN - La « Singapore Sun » a connu des débuts difficiles. Avec son pneu trop large et sa fourche longue, elle a été plus abîmée qu'améliorée en Asie avant que One Way Machine ne lui insuffle une seconde vie. Julian décide de redresser la situation en équipant la machine de pneus sculptés et d'une fourche de hill climbing. Il recouvre l'ancien réservoir Triumph et les pièces périphériques fabriquées à la main d'une bonne couche de peinture noire pour obtenir un contraste parfait avec les chatoiements du laiton. Aujourd'hui à Singapour, le fier propriétaire apprécie à sa juste valeur le fait que cette show bike puisse vraiment rouler.

89

IRON RIOT - Julian didn't make any compromises with the "Iron Riot". It's a motorcycle with a consistent design, based on a 16-year old Softail. It features a giant perimeter brake, a half-open primary drive and sporty stub handlebars above the fork bridge. Thanks to its streamlined DKW fuel tank, this metallic silver bike runs like a dream. The Iron Riot is not just a random assortment of parts. It's an industrial product with a consistent design, perfect finish and maximum functionality.

IRON RIOT - Keine Kompromisse ging Julian bei der Iron Riot ein. Auf Basis einer 16 Jahre alten Softail entstand ein in sich schlüssiges Motorrad – mit riesiger Perimeter-Bremse, einem halb offenen Primärantrieb und sportlichen Stummeln über der Gabelbrücke. Das metallisch-silberne Gefährt wirkt auch dank des schlanken DKW-Tanks wie aus einem Guss. Die Iron Riot ist kein wild zusammengeworfener Teile-Mix, sondern ein kohärent gestaltetes Industrieprodukt mit perfektem Finish und maximaler Funktion.

IRON RIOT - Pour la « Iron Riot », Julian ne veut pas de compromis. Sur la base d'une Softail de 16 ans, il fait naitre une moto cohérente, avec un gigantesque frein périmétrique, une transmission primaire semi-ouverte et des manches de sport au-dessus du pontet de fourche. Avec sa teinte argent métallisée et son mince réservoir DKW, la moto semble faite d'un bloc. La Iron Riot n'est pas un assemblage hétéroclite de pièces, mais un produit industriel conçu de manière cohérente, doté d'une finition parfaite et totalement fonctionnelle.

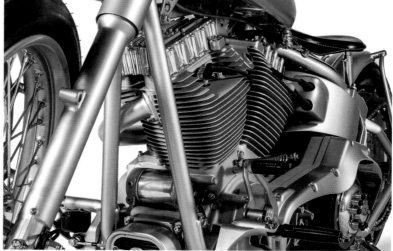

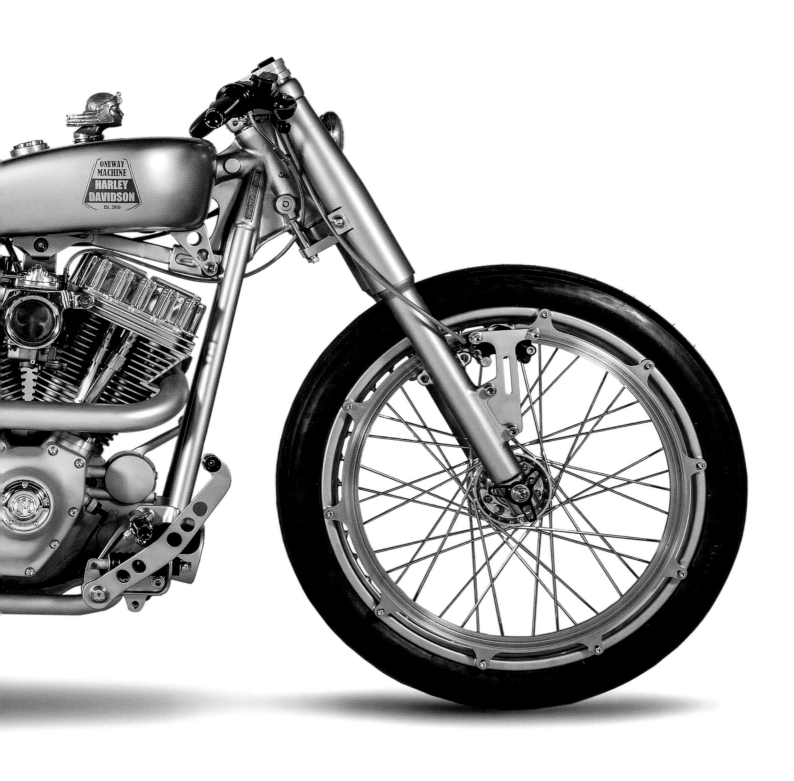

YOUNG GUNS
SPEED SHOP
1999 HARLEY-DAVIDSON DK

PHOTOS: LORENZ RICHARD

Few customizers have such fresh ideas and are as celebrated as much as the guys at Young Guns Speed Shop. So what's so special about Nik Heer and Fabian Witzig, the imaginative duo from the Lake Zurich region? They use their focus, lust for life, quick laps on motorcycles and alternative world views to combine features that are as different as water is to oil. A bike punk attitude and Swiss thoroughness combine to create an exciting product.

Nicht viele Customizer denken so frisch und werden so gefeiert wie die Jungs vom Young Guns Speed Shop. Was also ist das Besondere an Nik Heer und Fabian Witzig, dem ideenreichen Doppelpack vom Zürisee? Bei konzentrierter Arbeit, ihrem lustvollen Leben, forschen Motorradrunden und alternativen Weltsichten verschmelzen sie Pole, die sich sonst wie Wasser und Öl abstoßen: Bike-Punk und schweizerische Gründlichkeit werden zur spannenden Einheit.

Des transformateurs qui osent faire souffler un vent frais et sont autant célébrés que les gars du Young Guns Speed Shop, il n'y en a pas beaucoup. Alors qu'est-ce distingue Nik Heer et Fabian Witzig, le duo imaginatif du lac de Zurich ? Concentration au travail, joie de vivre, escapades dynamiques à moto, visions différentes du monde, le tout pour une fusion de pôles qui devraient se repousser comme l'eau et l'huile. Moto punk et rigueur suisse, un ensemble captivant.

99

1999 H-D DK - The 1200 Sportster is also an invention born of contradictions. A Japanese Mikuni carburetor supplies fresh air to the combustion chamber. A tank from a 1974 Husqvarna sits atop the clean frame. It took a lot of time to mount the Swedish piece onto the American steel, but the hybrid was a success. The smaller mounted parts, rugged tires and simple details like Magura levers and a motocross handlebar of the V2 conjure up thoughts of dirt tracks. In other words, this bike is also at home far away from the asphalt. Young guns rave about its genuine "badass" dirt bike feeling.

1999 H-D DK - Auch die 1200er Sportster wird durch Widersprüche belebt. In der Mitte des Motors sorgt ein japanischer Mikuni-Vergaser für frischen Wind im Brennraum. Auf ihrem gecleanten Rahmen thront der Tank einer 1974er Husqvarna. Es brauchte viel Zeit, um den schwedischen Fremdkörper am amerikanischen Eisen zu montieren. Doch die Symbiose ist geglückt. Dank reduzierter Anbauteile, groben Reifen und schlichten Details wie Magura-Hebeln oder dem Motocross-Lenker beflügelt der V2 vor allem schmutzige Gedanken. Denn auch fernab des Asphalts ist dieses Bike zu Hause. Die Young Guns schwärmen von echtem „Badass Dirt Bike Feeling".

1999 H-D DK - Les Sportster 1200 vivent de ces contradictions. Au milieu du moteur, un carburateur japonais Mikuni qui fait souffler un vent frais dans la chambre de combustion. Sur le cadre propret trône le réservoir d'une Husqvarna 1974. Il en aura fallu du temps pour monter un corps étranger suédois sur une machine américaine. La symbiose est pourtant réussie. Grâce à la réduction des éléments périphériques, aux gros pneus et aux détails simples comme les commandes Magura ou le guidon de motocross, le V2 suscite des envies de pistes sales. Car cette machine adore sortir de l'asphalte. D'ailleurs, les Young Guns parlent avec enthousiaste d'un vrai « badass dirt bike feeling ».

CHERRY'S COMPANY
DRAG QUEEN AND CHRONOS

PHOTOS: CHERRY'S COMPANY

Customization icon Kaichiroh "Cherry" Kurosu runs an unassuming workshop on a street corner in the heart of Tokyo. When customers walk in, they leave the loud street noise behind them. They immediately step into Cherry's world, with smells of hot metal, gasoline and engine oil. In the basement, Kaichiroh-san tinkers with classic motorcycles. One floor up, his bike frames hang on the wall. His family lives right above this floor. There's no doubt that working on bikes is Cherry's calling.

Die Werkstatt von Custom-Ikone Kaichiroh „Cherry" Kurosu liegt unscheinbar an einer Straßenecke mitten in Tokio. Wer sie betritt, lässt den Straßenlärm schnell hinter sich. Sofort taucht man in Cherry's Welt ein, die nach heißem Metall, Benzin und Motoröl riecht. Im Untergeschoss werkelt Kaichiroh-san an klassischen Motorrädern. Eine Treppe höher hängen seine Fahrradrahmen an der Wand. Darüber wohnt die Familie. Keine Frage, für Cherry ist Schrauben das halbe Leben.

L'atelier de l'icône de la moto personnalisée Kaichiroh « Cherry » Kurosu se voit à peine, sur un coin de rue au milieu de Tokyo. Une fois la porte franchie, le bruit assommant de la rue semble s'évanouir rapidement. On est tout de suite plongé dans le monde Cherry, qui sent le métal chaud, l'essence, l'huile-moteur. Au sous-sol, Kaichiroh-san bricole sur des motos classiques. Un escalier plus haut, ses cadres de vélos pendent au mur. La famille vit au-dessus. Aucun doute, pour Cherry, les boulons sont la moitié de sa vie.

DRAG QUEEN - Engines from Milwaukee are the origin of Cherry's passion. The "Drag Queen" is his homage to this passion. The 1948 Panhead equipped with racing slicks features typical Japanese overengineering and American patriotism. First, the hand-crafted frame is equipped with parts made from a complex sand casting to form the backbone of the racing bike. This bike features an engine cover proudly emblazoned with the American flag. There's no doubt about it. When a racer in the saddle of the Drag Queen, stretched out over the leather-covered tank, the racer is ready to take on the quarter-mile.

DRAG QUEEN - Motoren aus Milwaukee sind der Ursprung von Cherry's Leidenschaft. Mit der Drag Queen hat er dieser Liebe ein Denkmal gesetzt. Die Slick-bereifte 1948er Panhead beeindruckt mit typisch japanischem Over-Engineering und amerikanischem Patriotismus. Der handgefertigte Rahmen wird erst mit Teilen aus aufwendigem Sandguss zum Rückgrat eines Renners, dessen Motordeckel stolz das Star-Spangled Banner trägt. Ohne Frage – im Sattel der Drag Queen, über den mit Leder gepolsterten Tank gespannt, fühlt man sich für die Viertelmeile gewappnet.

DRAG QUEEN - À l'origine de la passion de Cherry, il y a les moteurs fabriqués à Milwaukee. La « Drag Queen » est un hommage à cette passion. La Panhead 1948 équipée de pneus slicks impressionne par sa conception inutilement complexe typiquement japonaise et son patriotisme américain. Le cadre fabriqué à la main est complété par des pièces coulées au sable, un procédé complexe, et devient ainsi la colonne vertébrale d'une machine de course dont le capot-moteur porte fièrement le drapeau américain. Aucun doute : sur la selle de la Drag Queen, sur le réservoir garni de cuir, on se sent fin prêt pour le quart de mile.

CHRONOS – Cherry looked to the past for inspiration in creating the "Chronos", a compact beast that only took two months until it saw the light of day. This Shovel/Panhead hybrid with large wheels, a springer fork and elegant retro styling, this bike is in the mold of old Boardtrackers. This time machine is an homage to the heroes of the previous century who raced across wooden tracks at full throttle with a healthy dose of courage. The name suits the bike perfectly. "Chronos" was the god of time in Greek mythology.

CHRONOS – Der Blick in die Vergangenheit inspirierte Cherry zur Chronos, einem gedrungenen Biest, das in nur zwei Monaten das Licht der Welt erblickte. Mit großen Rädern, einer Springer-Gabel und elegantem Retro-Styling zitiert der Shovel-Panhead-Mix die Linie alter Board-Tracker. Die Zeitmaschine huldigt Helden des vorigen Jahrhunderts, die mit Vollgas und einer gehörigen Portion Mut über hölzerne Pisten bretterten. Der Name passt dazu perfekt, spielt Chronos doch auf den Gott der Zeit in der griechischen Mythologie an.

CHRONOS – Cherry s'est inspiré du passé pour créer « Chronos », une bête trapue qui a vu le jour en seulement deux mois. Avec ses grandes roues, une fourche Springer et un élégant style rétro, ce mélange de shovelhead et de panhead évoque la ligne des anciennes board-trackers. La machine à remonter le temps rend hommage aux héros du siècle précédent qui sillonnaient des pistes défoncées, poignée dans le coin, avec une bonne dose d'audace. Le nom choisi est idéal puisque « Chronos » désigne le dieu du temps dans la mythologie grecque.

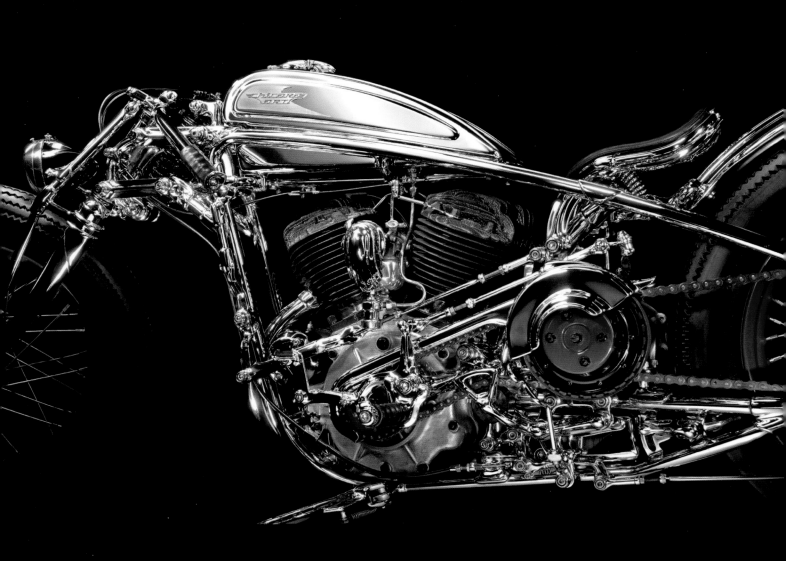

here's certainly no customizer more osessed with the idea of perfection than hicara Nagata. However, this reserved apanese man—a skilled graphic designer ho has been creating radical, one-of-a-kind kes for 10 years—hardly fits the mold of a ustomizer. Nagata has an astute mind and an esthete who combines the philosophy force, movement and physics in obsessive orks of art. His motorcycles aren't just a eans of transport. They're an expression of ure dedication. And his dedication knows bounds.

Es gibt wohl keinen Customizer, der mehr von Perfektion besessen ist als Chicara Nagata. Allerdings wird der Begriff des Customizers dem zurückhaltenden Japaner – ein gelernter Grafik-Designer, der seit gut zehn Jahren radikale Unikate auf die Räder stellt - kaum gerecht. Nagata ist ein Feingeist, ein Ästhet, der die Philosophie von Kraft, Bewegung und Physik in obsessive Kunstobjekte presst. Seine Motorräder sind keine Fortbewegungsmittel, sondern Ausdruck absoluter Hingabe.

Il n'existe sans doute pas de transformateur qui soit plus obsédé par la recherche de perfection que Chicara Nagata. Pourtant, ce Japonais réservé, designer graphique de métier et réalisant depuis une bonne dizaine d'années des pièces uniques sans compromis, n'est pas vraiment un transformateur au sens habituel. Nagata est un esprit raffiné, un esthète qui comprime dans ses objets d'art obsessionnels une philosophie synthèse de force, de mouvement et de lois physiques. Ses motos ne sont pas des moyens de locomotion, mais exprime le dévouement absolu, au-delà de toute limite.

ART ONE ·· Nagata's debut work bears the simple name of "Art One", because the rest speaks for itself. The 1939 flathead engine is surrounded by a double cradle frame with flat contours. The natural lines of the frame and hand-crafted mounted parts each vie for the attention of the observer. The observer's gaze is also drawn to copper cables, stainless brass and an abundance of polished details. It's easy to see why this work took a full 7 500 hours to complete.

ART ONE ·· Nagatas Erstlingswerk nennt sich schlicht Art One. Weil es für sich spricht: Den 1939er Flathead-Motor umschlingt ein flach geschwungener Doppelschleifenrahmen. Dessen organische Linien buhlen mit den von Hand geformten Anbauteilen um die Aufmerksamkeit des Betrachters. Das Auge bleibt auch an Kupferleitungen, edlem Messing und einer Fülle polierter Details hängen. Sie machen zumindest ansatzweise nachvollziehbar, dass in diesem Werk volle 7 500 Arbeitsstunden stecken.

ART ONE ·· La première œuvre de Nagata était baptisée simplement « Art One ». Car le reste n'a pas besoin d'explication : le moteur flathead de 1939 se love autour d'un double cadre berceau aux lignes plates. Avec les éléments périphériques formés à la main, les lignes organiques de la machine cherche à forcer l'attention du spectateur. L'œil s'arrête aussi sur les canalisations en cuivre, en laiton raffiné, et sur une multitude de détails polis. De quoi faire comprendre au moins à peu près qu'il a fallu 7 500 heures pour réaliser ce travail.

EHINGER
KRAFTRAD
MADE IN GERMANY

PHOTOS: DIRK WEYER

In the eighties, he traveled clear across Argentina, Chile and South Korea to track down classic motorcycles squirreled away in backyards and under tarps. Knuckleheads, Vincents, Indians and Moto Guzzi racers—most of them in a sorry state but always tied to tales of adventure. Uwe Ehinger's relics come from every era from the thirties to the seventies. He bought them from police departments, collectors and owners and then he brought them to Europe.

In den Achtzigerjahren reiste er quer durch Argentinien, Chile und Südkorea, um in Hinterhöfen und unter Planen klassische Motorräder aufzustöbern. Knuckleheads, Vincents, Indians oder Moto-Guzzi-Rennmaschinen, meist in bedauernswertem Zustand, immer aber verbunden mit abenteuerlichen Geschichten. Uwe Ehinger kaufte die Überbleibsel aus den Dreißiger- bis Sechzigerjahren von Polizeibehörden, von Sammlern oder Erben und brachte sie nach Europa.

Pendant les années quatre-vingt, il sillonne l'Argentine, le Chili ou la Corée du Sud, pour dénicher des motos anciennes recluses dans des arrière-cours et cachées sous des bâches. Des Knuckleheads, des Vincents, des Indians ou des machines de compétition Guzzi, la plupart du temps dans un état déplorable, mais toujours associées à des histoires incroyables. Uwe Ehinger rachète les restes de motos des années trente aux années soixante à la police, à des collectionneurs ou à des héritiers, et les ramène en Europe.

Today, the Hamburg native is one of the most well-known bike customizers in Germany with his company Ehinger Kraftrad. He forged his own style. Reduced, streamlined and made in Germany. Before he builds the custom bikes, he creates them virtually on his computer. In painstaking work, the Ehinger Kraftrad team enters all of the dimensions, textures and materials into a massive database.

Ehinger Kraftrad develops some exceptionally outstanding custom bikes on occasion. Motorcycles like the Speedster or the Chopper that capture the look sought by the entire scene.

Heute zählt der Hamburger mit seiner Firma Ehinger Kraftrad zu den bekanntesten Customizern in Deutschland. Er entwickelte einen eigenen Stil: reduziert, schlank und Made in Germany. Bevor seine Custombikes gebaut werden, entstehen sie virtuell am Rechner. In mühevoller Kleinarbeit pflegt das Ehinger-Kraftrad-Team alle Maße, Texturen und Materialien in eine gigantische Datenbank ein.

Von Zeit zu Zeit entwickelt Ehinger Kraftrad besonders außergewöhnliche Custombikes, Motorräder wie die Speedster oder die Chopper, die die Aufmerksamkeit der gesamten

Aujourd'hui, avec sa société Ehinger Kraftrad, ce Hambourgeois est un des transformateurs les plus connus en Allemagne et il a développé son propre style dont les maîtres-mots sont : réduction, amincissement et « made in Germany ». Avant de réaliser ses machines originales, il les fait naitre sur ordinateur. Grâce à un travail minutieux et long, l'équipe de Ehinger-Kraftrad gère une gigantesque base de données contenant toutes les cotes, les textures et les matières.

De temps en temps, Ehinger Kraftrad conçoit des motos qui sortent totalement de l'ordinaire. Des machines comme « The Speedster »

SPEEDSTER - Ehinger's Speedster is inspired by sleek grass track racers. One part of the frame serves as a gas tank, with the glimmering banana seat housing the motor oil inside. For a North German, an extreme bike also has to have an extreme engine. This led to the V-twin that looks like a knucklehead at first glance. Upon closer inspection, it's made of a stripped 1937 engine from a side-valve Harley-Davidson combined with custom-made OHV heads and an exposed valve train.

SPEEDSTER - Ehingers Speedster ist insiriert von schlanken Grasbahnmaschinen. Ein Teil des Rahmens dient als Benzintank, er glimmernde Banana-Seat bunkert das Motoröl in seinem Innern. Für den Norddeutschen muss ein extremes Bike auch einen extremen Motor haben. So besteht der V-Zweizylinder, der zunächst aussieht wie ein Knucklehead, bei näherer Betrachtung aus einem 1937er Rumpfmotor einer Seitenventil-Harley-Davidson, kombiniert mit selbst konstruierten ohv-Köpfen und offen laufendem Ventiltrieb.

SPEEDSTER - La Speedster de Ehinger est inspirée des motos allégées qui courent sur les pistes en herbe. Une partie du cadre sert de réservoir, le siège Banana brillant contient l'huile-moteur. Pour l'Allemand du Nord qu'est Uwe Ehinger, une moto de l'extrême doit avoir un moteur de l'extrême. Ainsi, le bicylindre en V, qui ressemble au premier abord à un knucklehead, est en fait une association d'un bloc nu de 1937, prélevé sur une Harley-Davidson à soupapes latérales, et de culasses à soupapes en tête et distribution ouverte, conçues par Ehinger.

...OPPER – The chopper combines the feeling of the seventies with an homage to the trailblazers of chopper culture from the West Coast of the United States. Legendary German thoroughness and skill is evident in the long-forked bike. Welding seams with exacting precision on the high-neck frame and the optimized 1947 knucklehead engine are classic hallmarks of bikes from Ehinger Kraftrad.

...HOPPER – Bei der Chopper trifft Siebzigerjahre-Lebensgefühl auf Respekt vor den Vorreitern der Chopper-Kultur an der US-Westküste. Dennoch ist dem Lang-gabler die sprichwörtliche teutonische Gründlichkeit anzumerken. Akribisch aus-geführte Schweißnähte am Highneck-Rahmen oder der optimierte 1947er Knucklehead-Motor sind typisch für Bikes von Ehinger Kraftrad.

...HOPPER – Quant au modèle « The Chop-per », il associe l'esprit des années soixante-six au respect dû aux précurseurs de la culture du chopper sur la côte ouest des USA. Il n'en reste pas moins que la rigueur germanique proverbiale se remarque sur cette machine à fourche longue. Les sou-ures très précises du cadre à long cou ou le moteur Knucklehead optimisé de 1947 sont caractéristiques des motos réalisées par Ehinger Kraftrad.

...HOTOS: BERND WESTPHAL

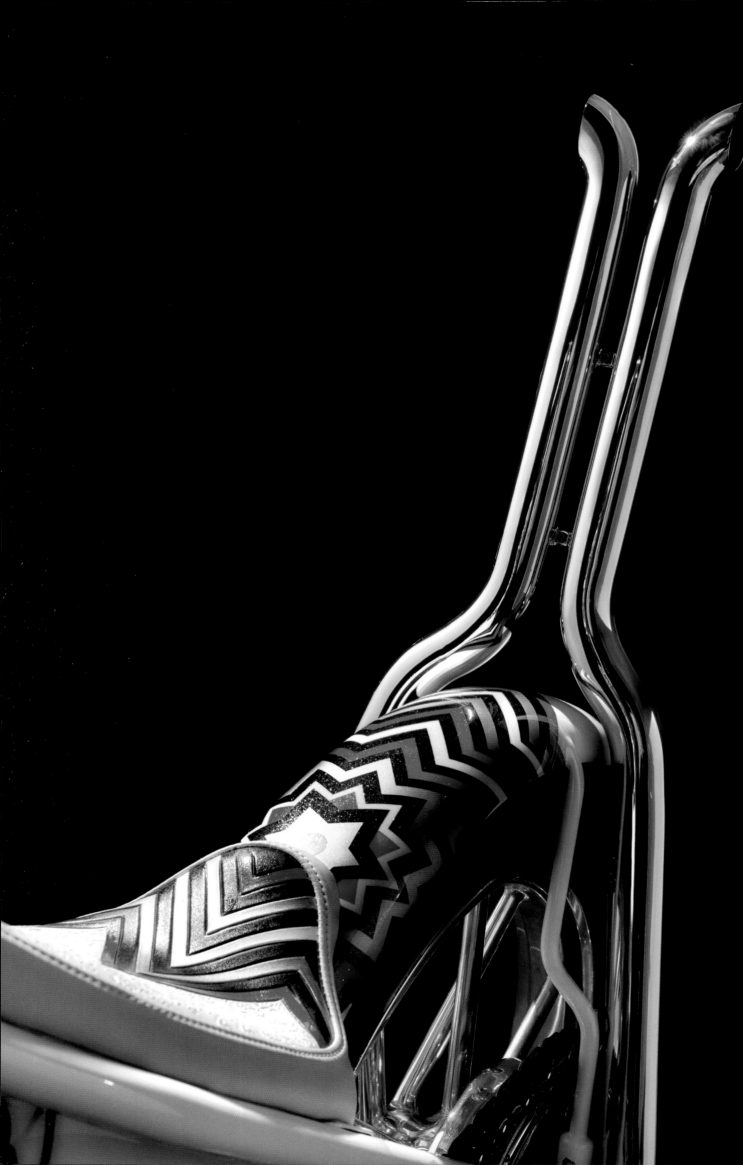

BATTLE
- THE -
KINGS

For most Harley riders, the purchase of a standard motorcycle is only the beginning. The first chapter in the relationship between man and machine, so to speak. To turn a little anecdote into an engaging story, personal modifications are often added to the common biography.

Für die meisten Harley-Fahrer ist der Kauf eines Motorrads von der Stange nur der Anfang. Sozusagen das erste Kapitel in der Beziehung zwischen Mensch und Maschine. Um aus einer kleinen Anekdote eine fesselnde Geschichte zu machen, werden oft persönliche Modifikationen zur gemeinsamen Biografie addiert.

Pour la plupart des conducteurs de Harley, l'achat d'une moto de série n'est qu'un début, le premier acte d'une liaison étroite entre un être humain et sa machine. Pour transformer un fait anecdotique en une histoire commune captivante, il faut se l'approprier en y apportant sa touche personnelle.

The Custom King competition accelerates the process of this convergence. The Motor Company, whose DNA has been imprinted with individualization since its establishment in 1903, has been awarding the Custom King title since 2015. All over the world, dealers and specialists are called up to give current bikes a new identity. Reason being that any Harley is like a blank canvas: It encourages its rider to come to terms with their reality and demands new ideas. The motorcycle as the mirror image of the ego in its saddle.

As proof of the unlimited possibilities hidden within every machine, hundreds of unique customized models have been rolled out already—fully faired racers, cool retro bikes, crunchy roadsters or untamed crossers. In the end, the people will crown their king.

Den Prozess dieser Annäherung beschleunigt der Harley-Davidson eigene Custom King-Wettbewerb.

Die Motor Company, deren DNA seit der Gründung 1903 von Individualisierung geprägt ist, lobt seit 2015 den Titel des Umbau-Königs aus. Weltweit werden Händler und Spezialisten aufgerufen, aktuellen Bikes eine neue Identität zu geben. Denn jede Harley ist wie eine weiße Leinwand: Sie fördert die Auseinandersetzung des Fahrers mit seiner Wirklichkeit und fordert neue Ideen. Das Motorrad als Spiegelbild des Ichs im Sattel.

Zum Beweis der unbegrenzten Möglichkeiten, die in jeder Maschine stecken, wurden bereits hunderte Unikate auf die Räder gestellt – voll verkleidete Renner, coole Retro-Bikes, knackige Roadster oder wilde Crosser. Am Ende krönt das Volk den König.

Le concours Custom King favorise ce processus de rapprochement. La Motor Company, dont l'ADN est marqué dès 1903 par la recherche d'identification individuelle, décerne depuis 2015 le titre de roi de la transformation. Concessionnaires et spécialistes du monde entier sont invités à donner une nouvelle identité à des machines modernes. Chaque Harley est alors comme une toile vierge qui incite le motard à chercher au fond de lui sa propre réalité, à y trouver des idées neuves. Ma moto, reflet de ce que je suis sur une selle.

Pour démontrer les possibilités illimitées que recèle chaque machine, des centaines de pièces uniques ont déjà été réalisées : motos de course intégralement carénées, machines rétros sympas, roadsters craquants ou crossers sauvages. À la fin, c'est le peuple qui couronne le roi.

YOU NEVER SEE A
MOTORCYCLE
PARKED OUTSIDE A
PSYCHIATRISTS
OFFICE

I don't ride a Harley to add days to my life, I ride a Harley to add life to my days

BIKES ARE LIKE WIVES...
IF IT AIN'T YOUR'S DON'T TOUCH

DON'T ASK TO RIDE MY BIKE AND I WON'T ASK TO RIDE YOUR  WIFE

FOUR
WHEELS
MOVE
THE BODY
- TWO
WHEELS
MOVE THE
SOUL

HOME IS WHERE YOUR HARLEY IS

REAL WOMEN RIDE MEN WITH HARLEYS

YOU DON'T STOP RIDING WHEN YOU GET OLD – YOU GET OLD WHEN YOU STOP RIDING

The best path through life is the open road

PUT SOMETHING EXCITING BETWEEN YOUR LEGS

THE BEST ALARM CLOCK IS SUNSHINE ON CHROME

THERAPY IS EXPENSIVE... WIND IS CHEAP

NEVER RIDE FASTER THAN YOUR GUARDIAN ANGEL CAN FLY

LIVING THE BIKE LIFE.

The "bike life" feeling connects people all over the world.
No matter where they come from or where they're going
and no matter what cultural background they have.
Harley-Davidson is at the center of a cultural movement.
It is the central element of the bike scene and brings people together for rallies and other events all over the world.
In recent years, Harley-Davidson has been taking on the
status of a luxury of analog in a world that continues to
become more digital. The brand inspires and it is inspired.
It's a riding machine. It embodies an authentic experience, appreciation, self-actualization and sensuality.
And celebration. Celebration of oneself. Harley-Davidson
means a vibrant attitude toward life. The epitome of freedom. Pure technique. Style. Fuel. Concentration.
A racing heart.

DAS INTENSIVE
GEFÜHL ZU LEBEN.

Das Bike Life Feeling verbindet Menschen weltweit. Egal,
woher sie kommen, egal, wohin sie gehen, was immer
ihr kultureller Hintergrund auch sein mag: Harley-Davidson
steht im Mittelpunkt einer kulturellen Bewegung, ist
zentrales Szeneelement, Motiv für Treffen und Events
rund um den Globus. In den letzten Jahren ist die Harley-
Davidson mehr und mehr zum analogen Luxus in einer
zunehmend digitalen Welt geworden. Sie inspiriert, sie
ist inspiriert. Ist Fahrmaschine. Steht für authentisches
Erleben, für Kennerschaft, für Selbstverwirklichung, für
Sinnlichkeit. Und für das Feiern. Das Sich-Feiern. Harley-
Davidson ist ein vibrierendes Lebensgefühl. Der Inbegriff
von Freiheit. Technik pur. Style. Benzin. Konzentration.
Herzrasen.

LE SENTIMENT
INTENSE DE VIVRE.

La moto est un art de vivre qui rassemble des gens du
monde entier. D'où qu'ils viennent, où qu'ils aillent.
Quelle que soit leur origine culturelle, Harley-Davidson
est au cœur d'un mouvement culturel, l'élément central
d'un univers à part, une raison de se retrouver et de faire
la fête partout dans le monde. Ces dernières années,
Harley-Davidson tend à devenir un luxe analogique dans
un monde de plus en plus numérique. Harley-Davidson
inspire et est inspiré. C'est une machine à rouler. Harley
est synonyme d'authenticité, de sensualité, Harley est
pour les connaisseurs, ceux qui veulent se réaliser.
Harley, c'est la fête. La fête pour soi-même. Harley-
Davidson, c'est la vie qui vibre. La liberté par excellence.
La technique pure. Le style. L'essence. La concentration.
Le cœur qui bat.

THE RIDE TO WHEELS AND WAVES

PHOTOS: LAURENT NIVALLE

On a typical day, only well-heeled old folks and tanned surfers mingle in the small French town of Biarritz. What is surely Europe's trendiest motorcycle festival has caused a stir for years now, providing a stark contrast in this tranquil resort town on the Bay of Biscay. It combines all cultures, all generations and all lifestyles under one banner. An expression of democracy and diversity fueled by gasoline and pure enjoyment of life.

Die französische Gemeinde Biarritz lässt normalerweise nur gut betuchte Rentner und braun gebrannte Wellenreiter aufeinander los. Doch für das eigentliche Kontrastprogramm im beschaulichen Badeort an der Biskaya sorgt nun schon seit einigen Jahren das wohl coolste Motorradfestival Europas. Es vereint alle Kulturen, alle Generationen und alle Stile unter einem Dach. Gelebte Demokratie und Vielfalt, befeuert von Benzin und purer Lebensfreude.

Normalement, la petite ville française de Biarritz est tout au plus un endroit où se côtoient des retraités plutôt aisés et des surfeurs bronzés. Pourtant, depuis maintenant quelques années, cette station balnéaire tranquille du golfe de Gascogne a trouvé une occasion de faire contraste avec son image habituelle en organisant le festival de moto sans doute le plus cool d'Europe. Une manifestation qui rassemble toutes les cultures, de toute génération et de tout style. La démocratie et la diversité en direct, sublimées par l'essence et une pure joie de vivre.

Even the journey there is an experience. The masses make their way to the Atlantic coast from near and far. They rumble across endless stretches of freeway or cruise through small fishing villages and rural roads to the melting pot of bike culture. The glint of the ocean is their constant companion. The technology might act up here and there, but that doesn't matter at all. With the sunshine in their face, the wind at their back and the anticipation of making new friends, even the most strenuous trip is sheer joy. After all, the wheels and waves are sure to make the trip worth it.

– –

Schon der Weg dorthin ist ein Erlebnis. Die Massen strömen aus allen Himmelsrichtungen zur Atlantikküste. Sie zermalmen die Kilometer auf der Autobahn unter ihren Rädern oder cruisen über kleine Fischerdörfer und Landstraßen zum Melting Pot der Zweiradkultur. Das Funkeln des Meeres ist ihr ständiger Begleiter. Vielleicht streikt hier und da die Technik, doch das ist völlig egal. Denn mit der Sonne im Nacken, dem Wind im Gesicht und neuen Freunden in Aussicht wird selbst die härteste Anreise zum reinsten Vergnügen. Wheels and Waves hat seine Versprechen bislang immer eingelöst.

– –

Rien que la route pour arriver là-bas est une aventure. Venant des quatre points cardinaux, les festivaliers arrivent en foule sur les bords de l'Atlantique. Ils avalent à fond les kilomètres d'autoroute ou prennent le temps de traverser les petits villages de pêcheurs par les routes de campagne pour arriver au grand melting pot de la moto. La mer qui étincelle sous le soleil ne les quitte jamais. Ici et là, il arrive que la technique se mettre en grève, mais quelle importance ? Avec le soleil sur la nuque, le vent dans le visage et la perspective de se faire des amis, même le voyage le plus dur pour arriver sur place est un pur plaisir. Jusqu'à maintenant, Wheels and Waves a toujours tenu ses promesses.

FROZEN FEW

PHOTOS: GÖTZ GÖPPERT

What happens when a traditional circuit race is crossed with a snowy winter landscape and a horde of crazy vintage bikers? The "Frozen Few" call their unusual hobby "the few, the fast and the frozen". Before the bearded racers meet in snowy Wisconsin, they modify their racing bikes themselves. Everyone in the gang has role to play. One can do the welding, another the upholstery work and another person can paint or do PR work. Harley-Davidson JDs from the 20s are proudly displayed in the workshop. They are equipped with an optimized 80-cubic inch engine, a reinforced frame, a lower solo seat and spikes for the tires. The Frozen Few call their stripped-down racing bikes "cut-downs".

Was kommt dabei heraus, wenn man einen traditionellen Rundstrecken-Wettbewerb mit winterlicher Schneelandschaft und einer Horde verrückter Vintage-Bike-Fahrer kreuzt? Nun ja, „The few, the fast and the frozen" eben. Bevor die bärtigen Rennfahrer im schneereichen Wisconsin zusammentreffen, bauen sie ihre Rennmotorräder eigenhändig um. Jeder Einzelne der Frozen Few füllt dabei seine Rolle aus: Einer kann schweißen, der Nächste polstern, ein anderer lackieren, oder er kümmert sich um die Pressearbeit. Mit Vorliebe stehen Harley-Davidson JDs aus den Zwanzigerjahren in der Werkstatt. Sie erhalten einen optimierten 80-cubic-inch-Motor, verstärkte Rahmen,

Qu'est-ce qui peut bien se passer quand on se retrouve devant une course traditionnelle sur circuit rond, dans un paysage enneigé, avec une horde de dingues de la moto vintage ? Ces gens s'appellent eux-mêmes les « Frozen Few » et ils ont donné à leur hobby original le nom de « The few, the fast and the frozen ». Avant de se réunir dans le Wisconsin enneigé, ces pilotes de course barbus construisent eux-mêmes leurs machines de course. Chaque membre de la troupe a un rôle défini. L'un sait souder, l'autre s'occupe de la sellerie, un troisième de la peinture ou des relations avec la presse. Dans l'atelier, leur préférence va aux JD Harley-Davidson des années vingt. Ils leur greffent un moteur

The style-conscious organizers are also picky about the location for the vintage snow racers. An industrial area from the early twentieth century is required to create an authentic vintage atmosphere. The show on bare ice is sensational, but the number of spectators is modest. Frozen Few member Mel Stultz explains why. "It's not easy to get people outside in these temperatures."

einen tiefergelegten Solosattel und Spikes für die Reifen. „Cut Downs" nennen die Frozen Few ihre minimalistischen Racer. Auch beim Austragungsort der Vintage Snow Races sind die stilbewussten Veranstalter wählerisch. Es muss schon ein Industriegelände aus dem frühen 20. Jahrhundert sein, um eine authentische Vintage-Atmosphäre zu kreieren. Trotz der sensationellen Show auf blankem Eis halten sich die Zuschauerzahlen im Rahmen. Dazu Frozen-Few-Mitglied Mel Stultz: „Es ist gar nicht so leicht, jemanden bei diesen Temperaturen nach draußen zu locken."

optimisé de 80 pouces cubes, un cadre renforcé, une selle solo abaissée et des clous pour les pneus. Ces machines minimalistes de course, les Frozen Few les appellent « Cut Downs ». Les organisateurs sont aussi très regardants quand il s'agit de choisir le site de leurs courses dans la neige. Il leur faut au moins un terrain industriel du début des années vingt pour créer une véritable atmosphère vintage. Malgré le spectacle sensationnel des courses sur la glace nue, le nombre de spectateurs est limité. Mel Stultz, membre des Frozen Few, a son opinion : « C'est vraiment pas facile de faire sortir les gens de chez eux par des températures pareilles. »

RACE OF GENTLEMEN
EAST AND WEST

PHOTOS: GÖTZ GÖPPERT

All eyes are on the are on the flag girl. Dressed in Harley Davidson service overalls, this blonde lady decides when the race will start. The two antique motorcycles roar to life as the starter's flag moves to the ground in a high arcing pattern. The rear wheels churn up meter-high jets of sand, and the smell of engine oil and burned clutch is in the air. For a moment, the spectators are taken back to the Roaring Twenties.

Alle Augen richten sich auf das Flag Girl. Bekleidet mit einem Harley-Davidson-Service-Overall, entscheidet die blonde Dame über den richtigen Zeitpunkt des Starts. Die beiden antiken Motorräder brüllen laut auf, als die Flagge zu Boden fliegt. Die Hinterräder wirbeln meterhohe Sandfontänen auf, es riecht nach Motoröl und verbrannten Kupplungsbelägen. Für einen Augenblick fühlen sich die Zuschauer in die wilden Zwanzigerjahre zurückversetzt.

Tous les yeux sont tournés sur la fille qui porte le drapeau. Revêtue d'une combinaison de mécano Harley-Davidson, la blonde décide du bon moment pour donner le départ. Les deux motos anciennes hurlent dès que le drapeau s'abaisse en faisant un grand arc de cercle. Les roues arrière projettent des fontaines de sable de plusieurs mètres, ça sent l'huile et les garnitures d'embrayage brûlées. Pendant un moment, les spectateurs se croient transportés à l'époque sauvage des années vingt.

Decked out in the style of the US hot rod tradition, over 100 vintage cars from 1934 and earlier and classic motorcycles built before 1947 are featured at the Race of Gentlemen East. The riders are wearing clothes from that era, the live music is period and the sprint races are as tough as nails. History is brought to life at Wildwood Beach in New Jersey.

Everyone who lives on the other coast can enjoy the Race of Gentlemen West at Pismo Beach in California, which boasts a combination of fine, white sand and a relaxed West Coast attitude.

Ganz im Stil der US-amerikanischen Hot-Rod-Tradition treffen sich einmal im Jahr über 100 Vintage-Cars bis Baujahr 1934 und klassische Motorräder, die vor 1947 gebaut wurden, zum Race of Gentlemen East. Die Fahrer stilecht gekleidet, die Live-Musik historisch korrekt, die Sprintrennen eisenhart. Am Strand von Wildwood im US-Bundesstaat New Jersey wird Geschichte lebendig.

Und für alle, die es nicht weit bis zur gegenüberliegenden Seite des amerikanischen Kontinents haben, findet im kalifornischen Pismo Beach das Race of Gentlemen West statt – auf feinem weißem Sand und kombiniert mit locker-leichtem West-Coast-Lebensgefühl.

Tout à fait dans le style de la tradition américaine du hot rod, plus de 100 voitures vintage fabriquées jusqu'en 1934 et de motos classiques construites avant 1947 se retrouvent une fois par an à l'occasion de la Race of Gentlemen East. Les conducteurs sont habillés dans le style de l'époque, la musique live est d'époque, les courses de sprint sont hyperdures. Sur la plage de Wildwood, dans l'État du New Jersey, l'histoire revit.

Et pour tous ceux qui ne sont pas loin de la côte opposée du continent américain, le site californien de Pismo Beach accueille la Race of Gentlemen West, sur le sable blanc et fin, dans l'ambiance légère et décontractée de la côte ouest.

BORN FREE SHOW

PHOTOS: DA GURU PHOTOGRAPHY

One of the world's coolest events for vintage choppers and classic motorcycles takes place 85 kilometers southeast of downtown Los Angeles. You know the Born Free Show has come again when the big ride around the Oak Canyon Ranch in Silverado starts on the festival grounds, when thousands of classic bikes fill the side roads and when Invited Builders each unveil their frenzy of chrome and metallic paint. The first pre-parties for Born Free start days ahead of time, such as at Cooks Corner or Feltraiger. This is why many visitors arrive even before the event starts. They enjoy the supercharged atmosphere and the dry heat.

Die wohl weltweit coolste Veranstaltung für Vintage-Chopper und klassische Motorräder findet 85 Kilometer südöstlich von Downtown Los Angeles statt. Wenn rund um die Oak Canyon Ranch in Silverado der große Run auf das Festivalgelände losgeht, wenn innerhalb kurzer Zeit Tausende von klassischen Bikes die Zufahrtsstraßen verstopfen und „Invited Builder" ihre Orgien aus Chrom und Flake-Lack enthüllen, dann beginnt wieder die Born Free Show. Bereits Tage vorher starten die ersten Pre-Partys, etwa im Cook's Corner oder bei Feltraiger. Viele Teilnehmer reisen daher frühzeitig an, sie genießen die aufgeladene Stimmung und die trockene Hitze.

La manifestation sans doute la plus cool du monde pour les choppers vintage et motos classiques a lieu à 85 kilomètres au sud-est de Downtown Los Angeles. Lorsque tout autour de l'Oak Canyon Ranch, à Silverado, commence la grande ruée vers le site du festival, lorsqu'en un minimum de temps, des milliers de motos classiques encombrent les voies d'accès et que les « Invited builders » dévoilent leurs orgies de chrome et de peinture métallisée, alors le Born Free Show peut vraiment débuter. Les premières pre-partys ont lieu quelques jours avant, par exemple dans le Cooks Corner ou encore chez Feltraiger. Beaucoup de participants arrivent en avance pour profiter de l'ambiance survoltée et de la chaleur sèche.

159

It all started with a small, one-day meet-up for classic choppers and antique motorcycles. With just a few hundred taking part. By the second year, Born Free had grown into a massive event. The two organizers, Grant "Large Hand" Petersen and Mike Davies, evidently found an immense niche to fill, drawing the champions from the customizing scene in California with their old-school concept. Even customizers from Japan, long-time admirers of the California scene, arrive in droves and transform Born Free into a world-famous event.

Angefangen hat alles als kleines, eintägiges Treffen für traditionelle Chopper und antike Motorräder. Mit ein paar Hundert Teilnehmern. Bereits im zweiten Jahr wuchs die Born Free zu einem riesigen Event. Die beiden Veranstalter Grant „Large Hands" Petersen und Mike Davis haben offensichtlich ein Vakuum gefüllt und mit ihrem Old-School-Konzept die Protagonisten der regen kalifornischen Customizing-Szene angelockt. Auch japanische Customizer reisen in Scharen an und machen die Born Free zu einer international anerkannten Veranstaltung.

Tout avait commencé par une petite rencontre d'une journée de choppers traditionnels et de motos anciennes, pour quelques centaines de participants. Dès la deuxième année, la Born Free s'est transformée en gigantesque manifestation. Les deux organisateurs, Grant « Large Hand » Petersen et Mike Davies, avaient manifestement comblé un manque et attiré avec leur concept old-school les acteurs du milieu très actif de la personnalisation et de la transformation en Californie. Même des transformateurs japonais qui ont toujours idolâtré le milieu californien sont venus en masse pour faire de cette Born Free un rassemblement reconnu au niveau international.

ON THE ROAD

PHOTOS: DA GURU PHOTOGRAPHY

Harley-Davidson. These two words promise freedom and adventure as well as fun and coolness. After all, this brand from Milwaukee is not only the embodiment of big-engined bikes, it also captures the aura of a rebel lifestyle that brings very different people together. Some hardcore bikers live and go all out for their brand. Others find new friends in the Harley community. Friends who stand by your side and who enjoy big, loud parties. For many, the Harley-Davidson experience means a breath of freedom from the constraints of everyday responsibilities. The feeling of being part of one big family brings them together.

Harley-Davidson. Diese beiden Wörter versprechen Freiheit und Abenteuer, aber auch Fun und Coolness. Denn die Marke aus Milwaukee steht nicht nur für großvolumige Motorräder, sondern auch für einen ausgefallenen Lifestyle, der unterschiedlichste Menschen miteinander verbindet. Mancher Hardcore-Biker lebt kompromisslos für seine Marke. Andere finden in der Harley-Community neue Freunde, mit denen sie ausgelassen feiern, die ihnen zur Seite stehen. Für viele bedeutet der Mythos Harley-Davidson schlicht ein temporäres Ausbrechen aus den Zwängen des spießigen Alltags.

Harley-Davidson. Ces deux mots promettent liberté et aventure, mais aussi fun et coolitude. La marque de Milwaukee n'est en effet pas seulement un grand constructeur de motos, elle est aussi synonyme d'un mode de vie à part qui relie des femmes et hommes très différents les uns des autres. Beaucoup de motards dans l'âme vivent pour leur marque, sans compromission. D'autres trouvent de nouveaux amis dans la communauté Harley, autant pour faire la fête et se défouler que pour s'entraider.

And all of them together have the desire to feel the wind whipping past their face.

The most fun comes from riding, tinkering and partying with friends. When a group of Harley fans hangs out on the weekend— whether it's on the road, in a club house, at a Harley dealer, at the bar, in the garage, at a bike show or in front of a camp fire—the Harleys are an essential part of their way of life.

Sie alle eint das Gefühl, Teil einer großen Familie zu sein. Und allen gemeinsam ist der Wunsch, sich den Fahrtwind um die Nase wehen zu lassen.

Am meisten Spaß macht es, gemeinsam mit Freunden zu fahren, zu schrauben und zu feiern. Wenn sich eine Gruppe Harley-Verrückter am Wochenende trifft, um zusammen abzuhängen – sei es auf der Straße, im Clubhaus, beim Harley-Dealer, in der Kneipe, an der Werkbank, auf der Bikeshow oder vor dem Lagerfeuer –, dann ist die Harley ein unverzichtbarer Bestandteil ihres Way of Life.

Pour beaucoup, le mythe Harley-Davidson, c'est simplement la possibilité de s'évader un moment des lourdeurs de la routine quotidienne. Tous sont unis par le sentiment d'être membres d'une grande famille. Et tous ont en commun le désir de sentir l'air leur fouetter le visage.

Ce qui les amuse le plus, c'est de rouler avec des amis, de bricoler, de faire la fête. Lorsqu'un groupe de dingues de Harley se retrouve le week-end pour passer du bon temps, sur la route, dans le club-house, chez un distributeur Harley, au bistro, autour d'un établi, dans un bikeshow ou autour d'un feu de camp, la Harley est l'élément incontournable de leur mode de vie.

us Harley-Davidson roar

VELODROM

PHOTOS: DA GURU PHOTOGRAPHY

In the 1920s, board track racing on oval courses of wooden planks was one of the biggest crowd pullers in American motorsports. In these events, based on the European velodrome for bicycle competitions, riders slugged it out in arenas dubbed "Motodromes" at the big national motorcycle championship races. In addition to drawing crowds of up to 80,000, the speed of the bikes increased continuously. The press soon dubbed the wooden racetracks "Murderdromes" due to the lack of safety measures and the severe accidents that resulted. The end of the board track era came in 1932. But the influence of board track racing can still be felt today in motorsports in the United States in American-style circuit racing with banked turns and a stadium atmosphere.

In den 1920-Jahren zählten Board-Track-Rennen auf meist hölzernen Ovalen zu den Publikumsmagneten unter den US-amerikanischen Motorsportarten. Angelehnt an europäische Velodrome für Fahrradwettbewerbe, wurden auf den „Motodrome" getauften Arenen die großen nationalen Motorradmeisterschaftsläufe ausgetragen. Damit kletterten nicht nur die Besucherzahlen bis zu 80 000 in die Höhe, auch die gefahrenen Geschwindigkeiten stiegen kontinuierlich an. Die Presse taufte die hölzernen Rennstrecken wegen mangelnder Sicherheitsvorkehrungen und daraus resultierender schwerer Unfälle bald „Murderdromes". 1932 kam das Ende der Board-Track-Ära. Doch bei US-typischen Rundstreckenrennen mit Steilkurven und Stadionatmosphäre ist der Einfluss der Board Track Races auf den amerikanischen Motorsport noch heute zu spüren.

Dans les années vingt du siècle dernier, les courses de board track sur des pistes ovales le plus souvent en bois comptaient parmi les compétitions motorisées qui attiraient le plus de public aux États-Unis. S'inspirant des compétitions européennes dans des vélodromes, des stades baptisés « motodromes » accueillaient les grandes courses nationales des championnats de moto. Ces événements non seulement réunissaient jusqu'à 80 000 spectateurs, mais les vitesses ne cessaient de croître. Bientôt, la presse donna le nom de « murderdromes » à ces pistes en bois, en raison de leur manque de sécurité et des accidents graves qui s'y produisaient. La fin de l'ère des board tracks sonna en 1932. Pourtant, dans les courses typiquement américaines sur pistes à virages relevés, dans une ambiance de stade, on ressent aujourd'hui encore l'influence des courses de board track.

Bicycle competitions in Europe used solid, outdoor concrete tracks. The ovals were usually 333 meters long, such as the ones in Bielefeld and Darmstadt, or 198 meters like the one in Singen on Lake Constance. Today they are ideal for show races with classic motorcycles. The historic Harley-Davidson board track racers without a transmission, suspension or brakes stand out in particular, just like back in the wild twenties.

In Europa setzte man für Fahrradwettbewerbe auf solide Freiluft-Betonbahnen. Die meist 333 Meter langen Ovale wie die in Bielefeld und Darmstadt oder Singen am Bodensee (mit 198 Meter) eignen sich heute perfekt für Showläufe mit klassischen Motorrädern. Dabei stechen vor allem die historischen Harley-Davidson-Board-Track-Racer ohne Getriebe, Federung und Bremsen heraus – ganz so wie in den wilden Zwanzigern.

En Europe, les courses de vélos étaient organisées sur des pistes de plein air en béton. Les ovales de 333 mètres de long, comme ceux de Bielefeld et Darmstadt, ou encore celui de Singen sur le lac de Constance (198 m de long) sont aujourd'hui parfaitement adaptés aux courses exhibitions réunissant des motos classiques. Et là, ce sont surtout les Boardtrack-Racers de Harley-Davidson qui se distinguent, dans des versions de course sans boîte de vitesses, sans suspension, sans freins, exactement comme dans les sauvages années vingt.

175

THE DISTINGUISHED GENTLEMAN'S RIDE

PHOTOS: AMY SHORE

Every last Sunday in September, dapper gentlemen starch their shirts, iron their pants, put on high-class ties and climb aboard their motorcycles. They flood the streets of countless major cities around the world on their beautiful classic bikes. All for a good cause.

The Distinguished Gentleman's Ride was created in 2012 by Australian Mark Hawwa. A stylish photo of actor Jon Hamm, the antithesis of a rebellious hell-raiser, inspired him to make the event for gentlemen. The old-school outing took place in Sydney as well as 63 other cities in parallel—a global phenomenon.

Jeden letzten Sonntag im September stärken geschmackvolle Gentlemen ihre Hemden, bügeln Hosen, binden feine Krawatten um und werfen dann das Bein über die Sitzbank ihrer Maschinen. Sie fluten auf klassisch schönen Motorrädern die Straßen unzähliger Metropolen rund um den Globus. Alles für eine gute Sache.

Der Distinguished Gentleman's Ride wurde 2012 vom Australier Mark Hawwa ins Leben gerufen. Ein stilvolles Foto des Schauspielers Jon Hamm als Don Draper - ein Gegenentwurf zum bösen Rocker - inspirierte ihn zur Herrentour. Die Ausfahrt alter Schule fand aber nicht nur in Sydney, sondern parallel in 63 weiteren Städten statt - ein weltweites Phänomen.

Le dernier dimanche de septembre, des gentlemen au goût sûr amidonnent leurs chemises, repassent leurs pantalons, nouent leurs élégantes cravates... et enfourchent leurs machines. Sur leurs belles motos anciennes, ils envahissent les rues d'innombrables métropoles du monde. Le tout pour une bonne cause.

La Distinguished Gentleman's Ride a été créée en 2012 par l'Australien Mark Hawwa. Cette idée de balade d'hommes à moto lui a été inspirée par une photo très stylée de l'acteur Jon Hamm, l'opposé du méchant rocker. Sydney n'est pas le seul endroit où se déroule cet événement à l'ancienne, puisqu'il a lieu en parallèle dans 63 autres villes, un phénomène donc devenu mondial.

Wearing fine threads on a motorcycle drew plenty of attention. And became an immediate success. The refined event is now used to collect donations and create awareness for men's health and cancer prevention. More than 50,000 participants per year and several million dollars raised are proof that tackling serious issues and enjoying a group bike ride do not have to be mutually exclusive.

Der feine Zwirn auf dem Motorrad sorgte für viel Aufsehen. Und wurde sogleich zum Erfolg. Denn das gesittete Happening wird seither genutzt, um Spenden zu sammeln und über Männergesundheit sowie Krebsvorsorge aufzuklären. Mehr als 50 000 Teilnehmer jährlich und viele Millionen Dollar sind der Beweis dafür, dass sich ernste Themen und gemeinsamer Fahrspaß auf dem Bike nicht ausschließen müssen.

Ces hommes en costume élégant sur leurs motos ont tout de suite attiré l'attention. Et le succès fut immédiat. Depuis, cet événement raffiné sert à collecter des dons et à favoriser l'information sur la santé masculine et la prévention des cancers. Plus de 50 000 participants chaque année et plusieurs millions de dollars démontrent que les sujets sérieux et le plaisir de faire de la moto ensemble ne sont en rien incompatibles.

SCENE SPRINTS

PHOTOS: DA GURU PHOTOGRAPHY

The new age custom scene has been fueled by the burning desire for ultra-cool, personalized motorcycles for several years. The mantra resembles a modern trinity. Vintage look, adventurous bravado and speed with style are at the top of the list. So there is good reason why traditional sprints have become established as a mix of these ideals in big scene events. Show business, baby!

Wheels and Waves, Glemseck 101, Café Racer Festival—all of these events focus on maximum speed. Professional racing drivers, customizers and amateur sprinters race to the horizon for an audience at the edge of their seats.

Wie ein Flammenwerfer befeuert die New-Age Custom Scene seit ein paar Jahren den Wunsch nach individuellen, hippen Motorrädern. Das Mantra gleicht einer modernen Dreifaltigkeit: Vintage-Look, abenteuerlustiges Draufgängertum und Speed mit Stil. Nicht ohne Grund haben sich deshalb klassische Sprints als Mix aus diesen Idealen im Rahmen der großen Szene-Events etabliert. Show Business, Baby!

Wheels and Waves, Glemseck 101, Café Racer Festival – bei all diesen Veranstaltungen geht es auch um maximale Beschleunigung.

Depuis quelques années, la scène « custom new age » a fait exploser la demande pour des motos branchées personnalisées. Le mantra évoque une trinité moderne : look vintage, envie d'aventure, vitesse avec style sont les trois exigences à l'ordre du jour. Ce n'est pas sans raison que les sprints classiques se sont établis sous la forme d'une fusion de ces idéaux dans le cadre des grands événements de la moto. Show business, baby !

Wheels and Waves, Glemseck 101, Café Racer Festival – tous ces rassemblements tournent autour de la recherche de vitesse maximale.

Sometimes on regulation bikes and sometimes on bikes modded to the moon. Quarter mile or eighth mile? Doesn't matter!

Wild paint, wide slicks and nitrous injection are admired alongside beautiful flag girls. On the short straights, however, the draw is the one-on-one duel. Man versus man. Or woman versus woman. Thousands of fans cheer as the smoking, roaring bikes and the riders give it their all. Everyone wins in the end.

Publikumswirksam rasen Profirennfahrer, Customizer und Wannabe-Sprinter auf mal biederem, mal bis ins Extrem gezüchtetem Material gen Horizont. Viertelmeile oder Achtelmeile? Egal!

Im Angesicht schöner Flag Girls werden wilder Lack, breite Slicks und Lachgas-Einspritzungen bewundert. Auf der kurzen Geraden liegt der Reiz allerdings im direkten Duell Mann gegen Mann. Oder Frau gegen Frau. Tausende Fans toben, wenn die qualmenden, brüllenden Maschinen und ihre Piloten alles geben. Gewonnen hat am Ende jeder und jede.

Pour le plus grand plaisir du public, les pilotes professionnels, les transformateurs et ceux qui voudraient bien les imiter foncent vers l'horizon sur du matériel tantôt banal, tantôt dopé à l'extrême. Quart de mile ou huitième de mile ? Peu importe !

Devant les jolies filles porte-drapeau, on admire les peintures dingues, les slicks larges et les injections de gaz hilarant. Mais sur la courte ligne droite, ce sont les duels qui passionnent, d'homme à homme, ou de femme à femme. Des milliers de fans s'agitent lorsque les pilotes donnent tout sur leurs machines fumantes et hurlantes. À la fin, tout le monde est vainqueur.

HILLCLIMB ON ICE

PHOTOS: DA GURU PHOTOGRAPHY

Hillclimbing is an event invented in the United States that involves overcoming an extremely steep slope—or at least getting as high up as possible. If that weren't difficult enough, events like Harley & Snow at the Ridnaun ski resort or at the Prennerhang in Ischgl require storming up the mountain on slippery snow. Riders are organized into various categories. Paddle tires, tracks and skis are prohibited; spiked tires and snow chains are allowed.

Beim in den USA erfundenen Hillclimbing geht es darum, einen extrem steilen Hang zu bezwingen oder zumindest möglichst weit nach oben zu kommen. Als wäre dies nicht schon schwierig genug, muss bei Veranstaltungen wie Harley & Snow auf der Skipiste Ridnaun oder auf dem Prennerhang in Ischgl der Berg auf rutschigem Schnee erstürmt werden. Schaufelräder, Raupen oder Ski sind verboten, Reifen mit Spikes oder Schneeketten dürfen verwendet werden. Gestartet wird in verschiedenen Kategorien.

Inventé aux USA, le hill climbing, appelé en français « montée impossible », consiste à franchir une côte extrêmement raide ou au minimum à monter le plus haut possible. Et comme si ça n'était pas assez difficile, il faut vaincre non seulement la pente, mais aussi la neige glissante, dans des courses comme la Harley & Snow, organisée sur la piste de ski de Ridnaun (Tyrol du Sud), ou au Prennerhang qui a lieu à Ischgl (Autriche). Les participants sont répartis en catégories. Les roues-pelles, les chenilles et les skis sont interdits, tandis que les pneus cloutés et les chaines à neige sont autorisés.

Viewing the spectacle keeps you on the edge of your seat, especially when watching Harley-Davidson stock bikes, Harley-Davidson performance bikes and the Open category without any displacement restriction, once the V-Twins start roaring, the wheels tear up the slope of solid ice and raise a fountain of snow shooting several meters in the air. Lit by floodlights, 100 to 170 participants each vie for the bikes modded as prizes for the events, thundering up the steeply rising ski slopes trying to reach the top. Those who have crested the slopes between the ice-covered mountains of Silvretta or the Stubai Alps have a right to be proud—of themselves and their Harley on Ice.

Besonders bei den Harley-Davidson Stock Bikes, den Harley-Davidson Performance Bikes und der Open Category ohne Hubraumbeschränkung stockt den Zuschauern der Atem, wenn die V-Twins kraftvoll dröhnen, sich die Räder in die pickelharte Piste krallen und eine meterhohe Schneefontäne aufwirbeln. Unter Flutlicht kämpfen sich die 100 bis 170 eigens für die Veranstaltungen umgebauten Bikes die stark ansteigenden Skipisten hinauf und versuchen bis auf den Gipfel zu donnern. Wer die Hänge zwischen den vereisten Bergen der Silvretta oder den Stubaier Alpen erklommen hat, der darf zu Recht stolz sein – auf sich und seine Harley on Ice.

Les Harley-Davidson Stock Bikes, Harley-Davidson Performance Bikes et la catégorie Open sans limitation de cylindrée sont les catégories qui coupent le souffle aux spectateurs lorsque les moteurs bicylindres en V grondent, que les roues s'accrochent à la piste très dure et projettent des gerbes de neige de plusieurs mètres de hauteur. Sous la lumière des projecteurs, les 100 à 170 machines préparées spécialement pour ces courses s'attaquent à des pistes de ski raides pour tenter de parvenir au sommet. Et ceux qui parviennent à dominer les pentes entre les montages glacées du massif de Silvretta ou des Alpes de Stubai peuvent à juste titre être fiers, d'eux-mêmes et de leur Harley on Ice.

WAGNER. NOT JUST A GRAND OPERA COMPOSER.

Riding 365 miles for the emancipation of women. More than one hundred years ago, Clara Wagner competed in the race from Chicago to Indianapolis on her Harley. And put all the other competitors, exclusively men, in their places. But having a Harley-Davidson doesn't just mean winning races. The stylish bikes from Milwaukee also exude freedom, rebellion and adventure, as in the legendary classic film Easy Rider. Harleys are also appreciated all by themselves. They've always been a popular subject for photographers, graphic artists and airbrush painters.

WAGNER. GROSSE OPER, EINMAL ANDERS.

365 Meilen für die Emanzipation. Vor mehr als 100 Jahren trat Clara Wagner im Rennen von Chicago nach Indianapolis auf ihrer Harley an. Und verwies alle anderen Teilnehmer, ausschließlich Männer, auf die Plätze. Mit einer Harley-Davidson lassen sich aber nicht nur Rennen gewinnen. Die stylishen Bikes aus Milwaukee stehen auch für Freiheit, Rebellion und Abenteuer, wie im legendären Filmklassiker „Easy Rider"... Oder einfach pur: Eine Harley-Davidson ist seit jeher begehrtes Motiv für Fotografen, Grafiker oder Airbrusher.

WAGNER. COMME UN GRAND OPÉRA, UN PEU DIFFÉRENT.

L'émancipation sur 365 miles. Il y a plus de cent ans, Clara Wagner participe sur sa Harley à la course Chicago-Indianapolis. Et finit devant tous les autres concurrents, tous des hommes. Mais une Harley-Davidson ne sert pas seulement à gagner des courses. Les machines du Milwaukee sont aussi synonymes de liberté, de rebellion et d'aventure comme dans le film légendaire Easy Rider. Mais les Harley-Davidson se suffisent aussi à elles-mêmes : elles ont toujours été des motifs recherchés par les photographes, les graphistes, les artistes d'airbrush.

GIRLS ON BIKES

PHOTOS: HARLEY-DAVIDSON

Harley-Davidson has proved to be a favorite among women with a love of motorsports from the very beginning. Even back when vehicle motorization was in its infancy, young ladies were climbing into the saddles of their Harleys—occasionally much to the displeasure of their male colleagues. In 1910, Clara Wagner won a 365-mile race from Chicago to Indianapolis on her Harley, ahead of all the male participants. And Amelia Earhart took part in races on her pink bike— winning almost every time.

In 1915, Avis Hotchkiss and her daughter Effie crossed the American continent on a V2 mount. Vivian Bales, an avid Harley rider, appeared on the cover of The Enthusiast as the first "Enthusiast Girl" in 1929. A decade later, Linda Dugeau and Dot Robinson

Harley-Davidson übt seit frühesten Zeiten eine Anziehungskraft auf motorsportbegeisterte Frauen aus. Bereits zu Beginn der Motorisierung schwangen sich junge Damen auf den Sattel ihrer Harley - nicht immer zur Freude der männlichen Kollegen. 1910 etwa gewann Clara Wagner auf ihrer Harley ein 360-Meilen-Rennen von Chicago nach Indianapolis vor allen männlichen Teilnehmern. Allerdings blieb ihr die Trophäe verwehrt - weil sie eine Frau war. Und Amelia Earhart bestritt Geländewettbewerbe auf ihrem rosa lackierten Gespann - und gewann fast immer.

1915 querten Avis Hotchkiss und ihre Tochter Effie den amerikanischen Kontinent mit einem V2-Gespann. In der Hauszeitschrift „The Enthusiast" erschien mit der passionierten Harley-Fahrerin Vivian Bale erstmals

Depuis les débuts, Harley-Davidson a exercé un grand attrait sur les femmes passionnées de sports mécaniques. Dès les prémisses de la motorisation, de jeunes femmes ont enfourché les selles de leur Harley, ce qui ne plaisait d'ailleurs pas toujours à collègues hommes. En 1910, Clara Wagner gagne sur sa Harley une course de 365 miles entre Chicago et Indianapolis, devant tous les participants de sexe masculin. Pour sa part, Amelia Earhart participe à des compétitions de tout-terrain sur sa monture peinte en rose et gagne presque toujours.

En 1915, Avis Hotchkiss et sa fille Effie traversent le continent américain sur leur V2. Vivian Bale, une pilote passionnée de Harley, fut en 1929 la première « Enthusiast Girl » à paraitre en couverture du magazine

founded the first women's motorcycle club, the "Motor Maids", in 1940. Today, women riding 300 kg Harleys or competing in motorsports are no longer a rarity. Examples abound, such as dirt track lady Tammy Jo Kirk, dragster rider Linda Jackson from Columbia or Annemarie Datzer from Germany.

But a Harley-Davidson allows for more than just winning competitions. The bikes from Milwaukee also exude sex appeal. No wonder that photographs in biker magazines often feature ladies in sexy clothes and Harleys with shining chrome side-by-side. While there are magazines like "Harley Women" for interested ladies, the scantily clad blonde is an integral part of the Harley lifestyle for traditional motorcycle magazines with mostly male readership.

1929 ein „Enthusiast Girl" auf der Titelseite. Und den ersten Damen-Motorradclub „Motor Maids" gründeten 1940 Linda Dugeau und Dot Robinson. Heute sind Frauen auf 300 Kilo schweren Harleys und im Motorsport keine Ausnahme mehr – man denke nur an die Dirt-Track-Lady Tammy Jo Kirk, die Dragster-Pilotinnen Linda Jackson aus Columbia oder Annemarie Datzer aus Deutschland.

Doch mit einer Harley-Davidson lassen sich nicht nur Wettbewerbe gewinnen, die Bikes aus Milwaukee stehen auch für Sex-Appeal. Kein Wunder, dass aufreizend gekleidete Girls und chromblitzende Harleys gerne zusammen für Biker-Magazine abgelichtet werden. Während es für interessierte Frauen Magazine wie „Harley-Women" gibt, zählt für die meist männliche Leserschaft traditioneller Motorradzeitschriften die leicht bekleidete Blondine zum Harley-Lifestyle.

interne intitulé « The Enthusiast ». En 1940, Linda Dugeau et Dot Robinson fondent le premier motoclub de femmes, le « Motor Maids ». Aujourd'hui, les femmes pilotant des Harleys de 300 kilos ou participant à des compétitions ne sont plus des exceptions. Pensons seulement à Tammy Jo Kirk, la lady du dirt track, aux pilotes de dragster comme la Colombienne Linda Jackson ou l'Allemagne Annemarie Datzer.

Les Harley-Davidson ne permettent pas seulement de gagner des compétitions : les machines de Milwaukee sont aussi synonymes de sexappeal. Pas étonnant que des filles habillées de manière provocante et des Harleys aux chromes rutilants soient souvent photographiées ensemble dans les magazines de moto. Pour les femmes intéressées, il existe des magazines comme le « Harley-Women », mais pour un lectorat composé le plus souvent d'hommes, la blonde légèrement vêtue est inséparable de l'esprit Harley.

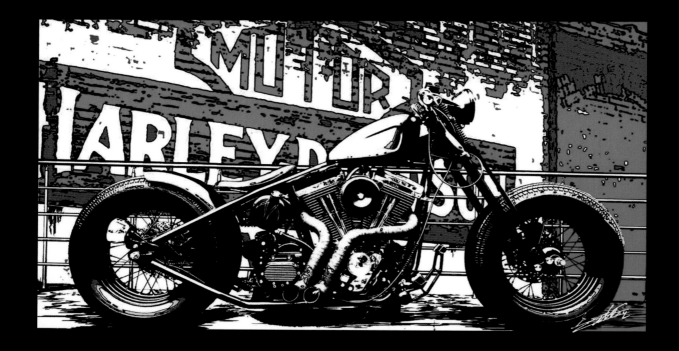

MOTORCYCLE ART

PHOTOS: WWW.BALESTRA-ART.FR

Harley-Davidson motorcycles have been the upper class of the motorcycle market for nearly a century. Exclusive dream bikes for fans of rebellious two-wheelers have been created in the US ever since. But there is a very special aura around the big V-Twins that has become known as the Harley-Davidson legend. A Harley-Davidson is not a soulless technical thing. It is an expression of human self-actualization.

Die Motorräder von Harley-Davidson zählen seit rund 100 Jahren zur Oberklasse auf dem Markt. Seit jeher entstehen in den USA exklusive Traumbikes für Liebhaber ausgefallener Zweiräder. Doch die großen V-Twins umweht darüber hinaus eine ganz spezielle Aura, die gemeinhin als „Mythos Harley-Davidson" bezeichnet wird. Eine Harley-Davidson ist kein seelenloser technischer Gegenstand, sondern ein Ausdruck menschlicher Selbstverwirklichung.

Sur le marché de la moto, les Harley-Davidson font partie du haut de gamme depuis une centaine d'années. Depuis toujours, des motos de rêve exclusives sont conçues et construites aux USA pour les amateurs d'engins à part. Mais les grosses V-Twins ont une aura toute spéciale, ce que l'on qualifie généralement de « mythe Harley-Davidson ». Une Harley-Davidson, ce n'est pas un objet utilitaire sans âme, c'est pour un être humain la façon d'exprimer sa personnalité et de s'épanouir.

t is no wonder, then, that the bikes from Milwaukee are perfect for works of art. Regardless of whether the piece consists of ilm, photography, graphics or airbrush vork, a Harley-Davidson is simply the perect motif and subject for many artists and raftsmen.

he cult film Easy Rider fit perfectly into ne times.

Kein Wunder also, dass sich die Bikes aus Milwaukee perfekt für die künstlerische Darstellung eignen. Ganz gleich, ob es sich um Filme, Fotografien, Grafiken oder Airbrush-Arbeiten handelt: Für so manchen Künstler und Kunsthandwerker ist eine Harley-Davidson einfach das perfekte Motiv und Objekt.

Perfekt hatte auch der Kultfilm „Easy Rider" in die damalige Zeit gepasst.

Il n'est donc pas surprenant que les motos imaginées à Milwaukee soient prédestinées pour l'expression artistique. Films, photo, dessins, graphisme, airbrush : pour un bon nombre d'artistes et d'artisans d'art, les Harley-Davidson sont tout simplement de parfaits motifs et objets de représentation.

Le film-culte « Easy Rider » aurait d'ailleurs aussi été parfaitement compris à l'époque.

When the road movie hit international the-
aters in 1969, it astonished an audience of
young movie-goers. Motorcyclists at the
time were a fairly conservative bunch and
expressed irritation at the open social criti-
cism and the "impractical and unsporty"
Harley Davidson Panhead choppers playing
a starring role alongside Peter Fonda, Dennis Hopper and Jack Nicholson. For many
young people, however, the movie stood for
freedom, adventure and an escape from the
conventions of everyday life. The movie's
two motorcycles, Captain America and The
Billy Bike, were the perfect getaway vehicles.
Incidentally, Easy Rider indirectly saved
Harley-Davidson from ruin by giving the
choppers a big boost in popularity.

Als das Road-Movie 1969 in die internationalen Kinos kam, ging ein Raunen durch das
in erster Linie junge Publikum. Die eher
konservativen Motorradfahrer reagierten
irritiert auf die offene Gesellschaftskritik
und die „unpraktischen und unsportlichen"
Harley-Davidson Panhead-Chopper, die
neben Peter Fonda, Dennis Hopper und Jack
Nicholson eine tragende Rolle in Easy Rider
spielten. Doch für viele Jugendliche stand
der Film für Freiheit, Abenteuer und Aus-
bruch aus dem spießigen Alltag. Die beiden
Motorräder, Captain America und The Billy
Bike, verkörperten die idealen Fluchtfahr-
zeuge. Und ganz nebenbei hat Easy Rider die
Marke Harley-Davidson indirekt vor dem
Ruin gerettet, da Chopper durch den Film
ungemein populär wurden.

Lorsqu'il sort dans les salles en 1969, ce
« road movie » suscite les murmures dans
un public essentiellement jeune. Les motards Plutôt conservateurs sont irrités par
cette critique ouverte de la société et les
« panhead choppers » Harley-Davidson,
« ni pratiques, ni sportives », qui jouent un
rôle de premier plan dans le film, aux côtés
de Peter Fonda, Dennis Hopper et Jack
Nicholson. À l'inverse, pour beaucoup de
jeunes, le film est synonyme de liberté et
d'aventure et est un pavé dans la mare du
quotidien banal de l'époque. Les deux motos,
Captain America et The Billy Bike, incarnent
l'idéal de l'évasion. Accessoirement, Easy
Rider a indirectement sauvé la marque
Harley-Davidson de la ruine, en étant à l'origine de l'incroyable popularité des choppers.

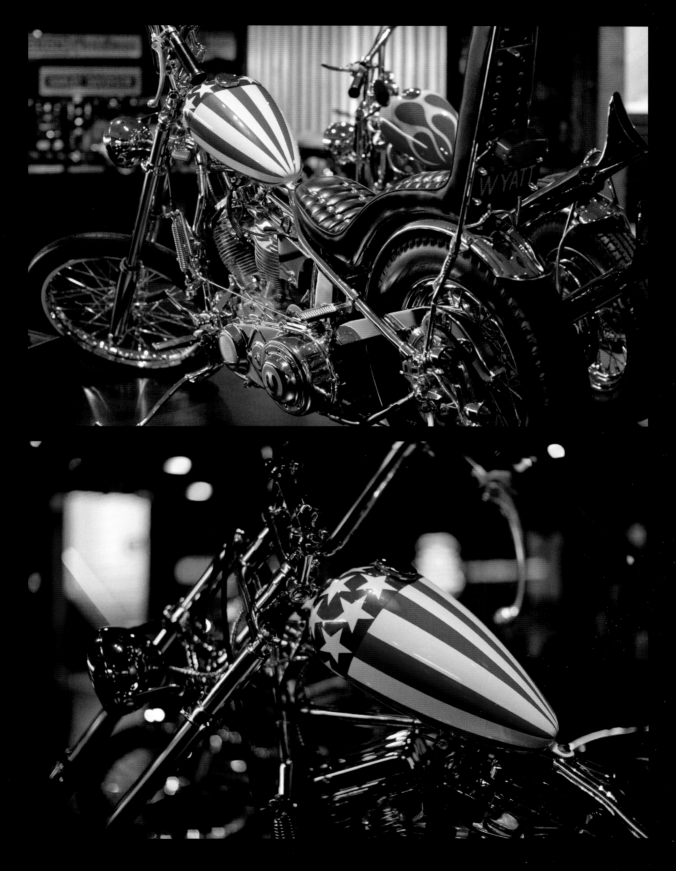

ART & GIRLS

IMPRINT

© 2020 teNeues Media GmbH + Co. KG, Kempen

Second Printing

PUBLISHER
teNeues Media GmbH & Co. KG

**EDITOR-IN-CHIEF /
CREATIVE DIRECTOR**
Michael Köckritz

ART DIRECTION
Carolin Freitag
ramp/studio

GRAPHIC DESIGN
Christina Ströbele, Franziska Wolf
ramp/studio

ILLUSTRATION
Milica Vezmar Basara
ramp/studio

EDITORIAL STAFF
Dirk Mangartz, Sven Wedemeyer,
Philipp Wente

PHOTO EDITOR
Antonietta Procopio

PROJECT MANAGEMENT
Marc C. Röder
ramp.space GmbH & Co. KG

EDITORIAL MANAGEMENT
Stephanie Rebel and Pit Pauen
teNeues Media GmbH & Co. KG
Marc C. Röder
ramp.space GmbH & Co. KG

TRANSLATION
STAR Software, Translation, Artwork,
Recording GmbH. www.star-group.net

COPYEDITING GERMAN
Claudia Jürgens

PREPRESS
Jens Grundei
teNeues Media GmbH & Co. KG

PRODUCTION
Dieter Haberzettl,
teNeues Media GmbH & Co. KG

**PUBLISHED BY
TENEUES PUBLISHING GROUP**

teNeues Media GmbH & Co. KG
Am Selder 37, 47906 Kempen, Germany
Phone: +49 (0)2152 916 0
e-mail: books@teneues.com

Press department: Andrea Rehn
Phone: +49 (0)2152 916 202
e-mail: arehn@teneues.com

Munich Office
Pilotystraße 4, 80538 Munich, Germany
Phone: +49-(0)89-90 42 13-200
e-mail: bkellner@teneues.com

Berlin Office
Mommsenstraße 43, 10629 Berlin, Germany
Phone: +49-(0)152 08 51 10 64
e-mail: ajasper@teneues.com

teNeues Publishing Company
350 7th Avenue, Suite 301,
New York, NY 10001, USA
Phone: +1-212-627-9090
Fax: +1-212-627-9511

teNeues Publishing UK Ltd.
12 Ferndene Road, London SE24 0AQ, UK
Phone: +44 (0)20 3542 8997

teNeues France S.A.R.L.
39, rue des Billets, 18250 Henrichemont,
France
Phone: +33 (0)2 48 26 93 48
Fax: +33 (0)1 70 72 34 82

www.teneues.com

ISBN: 978-3-96171-023-2
Library of Congress Control Number:
2017942038
Printed in the Czech Republic by
Tesinska Tiskarna AG

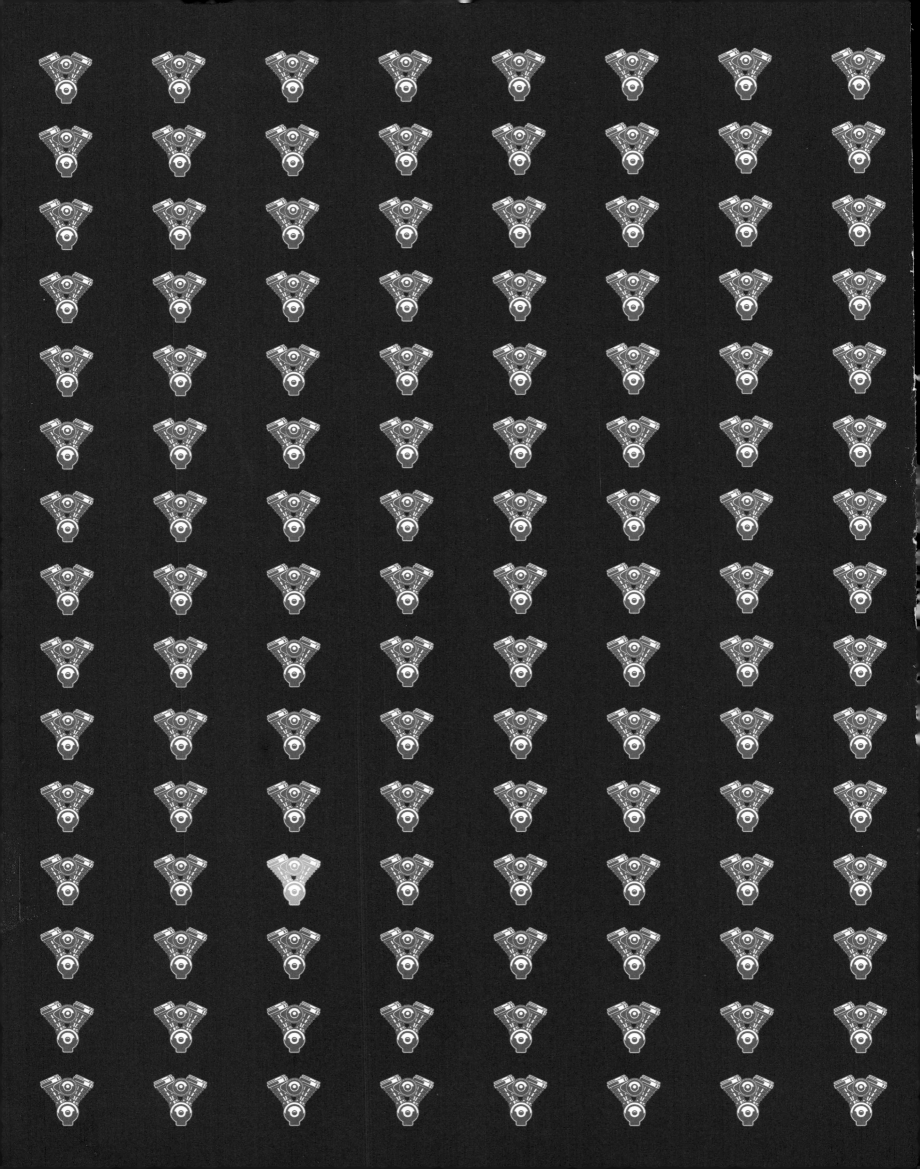